Celia
Gruwell
July 6, 1987

HOW TO FEEL
GREAT
ABOUT BEING A
MOTHER

HOW TO FEEL
GREAT
ABOUT BEING A
MOTHER

AMY HARDISON

Deseret Book Company
Salt Lake City, Utah

First printing February 1987

Library of Congress Cataloging-in-Publication Data

Hardison, Amy, 1959–
    How to feel great about being a mother.

    Bibliography: p.
    Includes index.
    1. Motherhood.   2. Self-actualization (Psychology)
3. Mothers—Religious life.   I. Title.
HQ759.H27 1987   306.8'743   86-29349
ISBN 0-87579-073-9

*To Steve, who honors and supports
me as a mother.*

CONTENTS

INTRODUCTION

*M*otherhood is a unique profession. It offers no monetary rewards, no bonuses, no raises, and no promotions. Mothers never receive days off, sick leave, or time-and-a-half pay for weekends and holidays. There is little external recognition. No one evaluates a mother's efforts and gives her a reward for outstanding performance. Few statues are raised, universities renamed, degrees given, or medals of honor awarded for a mother's lifetime of twenty-four-hour, on-call service. Indeed, the plaudits of mankind are few.

However, that's not to say that there are no rewards. There are rewards, but they are small in nature, as small as a baby's smile and a toddler's kiss. They are as small as a parent-teacher conference when a teacher says your child behaves well and demonstrates desire and effort. And they are as small as watching your five-year-old give a talk in Primary, the first one she has prepared herself. The reward does not diminish even though she says Joseph Smith "cancellated" the golden plates. These are the rewards of motherhood. They are small in nature and unacclaimed by the world. In fact, they are silent to all but the mother, who, like Mary the mother of Jesus, ponders them in her heart, and there receives joy.

The silent rewards of motherhood are internal rewards. They come from within. In fact, most of the essential aspects of motherhood also come from within. The love, enjoyment, dedication, and ability to meet the demands of a physically and emotionally taxing career must come from deep within a woman's heart. For this reason, a woman needs inner strengths from which to draw. She needs inner reserves of personal satisfaction, purpose and direction, excellence and fulfillment, happiness, and spirituality. These things bring joy into womanhood and transform motherhood into the most rewarding of professions.

DEVELOPING PERSONAL SATISFACTION

*I*n some aspects, mechanical objects have an advantage over human beings. They come with installation instructions, use-and-care manuals, and guarantees. Human beings, on the other hand, enter the world with none of these instructions. Perhaps it would be easier if they did. For instance, it might be helpful if a baby, like a new automobile, came with a window sticker that read as follows:

"This model is a unique special edition. Like all models, it is equipped with standard features like two-lung power, double bawl bearing, a water-cooled exhaust, and changeable seat covers. However, it is unlike any other model in its coloring, interior, and on-the-road manageability. There may be similar models made, but this one will never be duplicated. Keep this in mind for servicing. For this model to run smoothly, do not let the tank become completely empty as the engine tends to growl. Special care is required to keep this model clean and shiny. The exterior should be washed frequently (remember to clean behind the hubcaps) and dried thoroughly. Frequently wax with love. To keep the interior clean, do not bring in trash and garbage, for it is difficult to remove. If you have questions about keeping this model in top running condition, please consult manufacturer."

It would be helpful for human beings to have installation instructions for a baby's homecoming, trouble-shooting guides for misbehaving children, or before-you-call-a-repairman instructions for the sick. However, the most valuable kind of instructions or warranty would undoubtedly be the satisfaction guarantee.

The satisfaction guarantee is given in hopes of creating a satisfied (and thus repeat) customer. This guarantee ensures that if the product has flaws, or if it doesn't perform as it should, it can either be exchanged for a new product or have its purchase price refunded. Unfortunately, human beings don't come with such a guarantee. If we aren't satisfied with our appearance, we can't exchange ourselves for a new, flawless product. If we aren't satisfied with the way we performed a certain task or the way we interacted with our children, we can't demand a refund of those minutes. Personal satisfaction for human beings cannot be guaranteed by slips of paper or written words. Personal satisfaction must come from within.

Developing inner satisfaction is a difficult task for many people. Perhaps society is partially to blame for this. In today's world, improvement is status quo. Products are constantly being made bigger, better, or new and improved. Each year, laundry products get clothes whiter and brighter and cars have better performance and gas mileage. Food has a better flavor, less preservatives, or a new and improved recipe. This obsession for improvement also extends beyond products to people.

Today, it is difficult to be too rich or too thin, too successful or too beautiful, too organized or too efficient. Even within the Church, many women feel they can never give enough service, preserve enough peaches, spend enough time with their children, and keep their homes neat enough. This feeling that no effort is enough and that we should always be a little better and do a little more in order to be okay is a dangerous one for it makes personal satisfaction nebulous and unattainable. With such thinking, personal satisfaction becomes like the mirage of water we see on a road when driving on a hot day. No matter how far we drive, the water is always in the distance—just a little beyond wherever we are.

The first step in transforming personal satisfaction into an attainable attribute is learning to recognize the sources of dissatisfaction in our lives. Once we recognize them, we can then eliminate them.

1st step

Comparison Vision

By nature or necessity, many of us are comparative shoppers. We check the unit pricing at the grocery store to make sure the thirty-two-ounce box of Cheerios is a better buy than the twenty-four-ounce package. We compare one bank to another to discover which will return more interest on our money. And we go to each dress shop and department store in a shopping mall to ensure we are getting the most beautiful dress we can for the least amount of money. When we make large purchases—such as major appliances, furniture, cars, or homes—we are even more particular about comparing features, quality, style, and price.

This habit of comparing features and qualities is not limited to material goods but is too often extended to people. We compare our children to their siblings, our husbands to our brothers-in-law, one friend to another, and most frequently, ourselves to everyone else. However, people are not merchandise and should not be valued or dismissed because they have or lack certain traits and abilities. People are complex, multifaceted individuals, each possessing different qualities and strengths. We are not the same on the inside or out—nor are we meant to be. Each person was purposely created by God with different strengths and weaknesses. This is made clear in a revelation given to Joseph Smith: "For all have not every gift given unto them; for there are many gifts, and to every man is given a gift by the Spirit of God. To some is given one, and to some is given another, that all may be profited thereby." (D&C 46:11–12.) This scripture states that we all have different strengths and talents. And it gives the reason why—"that all may be profited thereby." It is because of our differences that we complement each other.

If this were not so, and if each person's strengths were the same as every other person's, life would be lopsided and incomplete. I learned this lesson several years ago when I was a Beehive advisor in the Young Women program. The Young Women president had planned a picnic for all the girls. She asked each of the advisors to bring a potluck item to accompany the hot dogs and buns the ward was providing. The day of the picnic, I prepared a large macaroni salad and carefully covered it with foil. That evening, I placed my bowl on the table with seven other large, foil-topped bowls. When we sat down to eat, we each unveiled our culinary contribution and beheld eight large bowls of macaroni salad.

Each of us had offered our contribution to the picnic and each had been the same. There was no variety, no individuality, and no outstanding favorites. In fact, it was a very boring spread. Similarly, if everyone's talents and abilities were the same, life would lack variety, uniqueness, and excellence. It would be very boring. Moreover, some very important qualities and abilities would be lacking.

Nevertheless, we continue to disregard the importance of our own unique qualities and frequently compare ourselves to others. This is especially dangerous if we base our self-esteem on the conclusions of the comparisons. Consider for instance what happens when we compare ourselves with another person and determine we come out the best of the matchup. We congratulate ourselves, chalk up a personal triumph, and elevate our self-esteem. However, our personal triumph rests in a very precarious position, for we can suddenly be thrust into a new comparison and our triumph along with our feelings of adequacy and self-approval can be snatched away as easily as they were obtained. When we base our self-worth on comparisons, we are forever shifting from worthwhile to worthless, depending on whom we are comparing ourselves with.

If we are in the habit of comparing ourselves to others, we will generally spend most of our time on the worthless end of the scale, for in making comparisons we are dissecting a character and making judgments on one trait to which we have momentarily granted supreme importance. And whom do we choose to include in this comparison? Ourselves and someone else who has the trait in enough abundance that we are aware of it. In these cases, we frequently come out the loser, and then we feel dissatisfied and inferior. Wallowing in feelings of inferiority, we forget that there is more to a person than a group of isolated traits. It is in the unique selection and arrangement of talents and traits that a person becomes an individual.

It is hard to remember this when engaged in comparing ourselves with others. How well I realized this during a recent trip to the grocery store. As I pushed the cart down the aisles, I passed a couple of large tables piled with books. The magnetic power of the words *Clearance Sale* attracted my cart, and I was compelled to turn toward the tables for just a few moments of browsing.

With great effort, I passed by the Strawberry Shortcake books that were marked half of what they had been marked before Christmas. I resisted the urge to buy *Cookie Monster and the Cookie Tree* in order to save it as a gift for some future birthday party my daughter would surely be invited to. And I even managed to keep the cookbooks out of my cart. But browsing moments turned into several minutes when I discovered *The Celebrities Fitness and Weight Book.* I became obsessed with finding the celebrities who were my height, discovering how much they weighed, and comparing their weight to mine. I became so mesmerized with my task that I muttered "In a minute" three hundred times to my children's demands of "Let's get going!" and even eventually gave them permission to go down the toy aisle. Ten minutes later, I put down the book, pulled in my stomach, and walked away in despair, wondering how I could lose ten pounds.

I gradually filled my cart, squishing my baby between rolls of paper towels and disposable diapers and forcing my older children to abandon their ride and walk. Soon my cart was so full that only an experienced grocery shopper could creatively stack the fruit so it wouldn't topple off and arrange slots for bread without leaving it flattened and dented. But my mind was even more full. I was overflowing with thoughts of dissatisfaction and inferiority. I had engaged in the game of comparative thinking, and I had lost. I had dissected my character and my person, isolated the trait of being thin, and given it supreme importance. I had dismissed the importance of all other qualities and attributes. In essence, I went to a picnic and valued only macaroni salads. I longed to be a macaroni salad, and I felt discontent, depressed, and inferior for being a Jell-O salad.

I learned through personal experience the great tragedy of comparative thinking. It undermines our self-worth, destroys our happiness, and diverts our energy and creativity to channels of negative thought. It can even distort to unrecognizable proportions the purpose and essence of life. Epictetus, a Greek philosopher, realized this and said: "How can I any longer lay claim to right principles, if I am not content with being what I am, but am all aflutter about what I am supposed to be?"[1]

Another evil of comparison thinking is that it often leads to imitation, but imitation rarely leads to satisfaction, especially when done at the expense of our own uniqueness. The story is told of one lecturer who learned this the hard way. This lecturer had frequently been requested to speak at a banquet at a nudist colony, but had always politely refused. Because of the persistent requests, he finally agreed, though nervous and uncomfortable about doing so. When he arrived at the nudist colony, he was greeted by large numbers of unclad men and women. He was shown around the colony and given a room where he could prepare himself for dinner.

Upstairs in the room, he felt there was nothing he could do except face the fact that he was expected to divest himself of his clothing. Embarrassed and uncomfortable he removed his and upon hearing the dinner bell, marched down to the banquet room. To his horror, he discovered that the colonists had all donned formal attire in deference to the speaker.[2]

Like this lecturer, we sometimes divest ourselves of our own uniqueness and individuality in order to imitate others, but imitation of this kind rarely gives us the result we hope for. I discovered this for myself at church one Sunday when I met a woman I thought was strikingly beautiful. Her eyes seemed to sparkle and light up her face. As I spoke with her, I scrutinized the way she had used eye shadow to bring out this beauty and committed it to memory. My admiration turned to imitation, and I bought the same color eye shadow and applied it as she had done. Although I didn't think the result was quite as striking, I continued to apply the eye shadow as she had done. Several months later I learned about color draping. I learned that, depending on a woman's coloring, there are particular colors of makeup and clothing that are more flattering than others. I then realized how unflattering my imitation had been. I had forsaken my own uniqueness and the results had been disastrous.

Dr. Wayne Dyer, a noted psychologist and author, explains

why disastrous results generally follow imitation. He says: "No one is even remotely like you in terms of your innermost feelings, thoughts, and desires. If you accept this notion, then you will want to take a hard look at why you would use anyone else's example as a reason for your doing or not doing anything."[3] It is because of this God-given uniqueness that we should consider our individual worth and refrain from the injurious practice of comparison thinking.

Unrealistic Expectations

Somewhere, somehow, there might be a supermother. A supermother is a mother who awakens her family with a smile on her face, immaculately applied makeup, and brushed hair, even when she's been up half the night with a sick baby. She then serves her family a hot breakfast of homemade whole wheat bread, bacon and eggs, and freshly squeezed orange juice—never cold cereal. Of course, in the supermother's home, each child's bed is made and each room is cleaned before the children leave ten minutes early to catch the school bus. The rest of the supermother's morning is spent cleaning her house, teaching her preschooler to read, playing intellectually stimulating games with her baby, making dinner for a ward member who is sick, and working on her four-generation group sheets.

During the afternoon, the supermother bakes cookies for her children—and never once takes a taste. She exercises aerobically, has a personal study session, makes a gourmet dinner for her family, and does the laundry without coming up with stray socks. She also greets the children with undivided attention when they come home from school, coaches a Little League softball team, and returns home in time to apply fresh makeup and perfume before cheerfully greeting her husband. A supermother's children cheerfully go to bed at 7:30, right after fifteen minutes of family scripture reading. The rest of the evening, the supermother devotes herself entirely to her husband. A supermother never has headaches, cramps, or postpartum depression. Her children never bicker, have runny noses, forget their homework, or wear clothes that don't match. Her furniture is never dusty and her windows are always shiny and spotless. Everything is perfect.

Somewhere, somehow, there might be such a super-mother—but I doubt it. Instead, there are thousands of mothers struggling to be supermothers, but not quite living up to the supermother standards they have so optimistically set. This discrepancy between expectancy and performance is another source of personal dissatisfaction. In many cases, the real culprit is not behavior, but unrealistic expectations.

For many women, the unrealistic expectations of motherhood begin when they are expecting their first baby. I know that from the first suspicion of pregnancy, I created utopian dreams of both motherhood and expectant mother-hood. Neither have been as easy or peaceful as I had imagined. I had envisioned pregnancy as a time to sew baby clothes, decorate a nursery, and choose names. Surely I too would have that glow of motherhood my husband admired in expectant women. Soon my face did have a glow, but it was a green one. Unending bouts with twenty-four-hour morning sickness left me with little desire or energy to sew, wallpaper, or paint. Any energy I did have seemed to be spent mustering enough courage to face the task of making (and smelling) dinner. Surely, I should have realized at this point that a mother's expectations and actual motherhood don't always coincide.

Nevertheless, I remained optimistic and held on to my quixotic expectations. In fact, I created a whole set of new ones as I cradled my newborn daughter. I would never become angry with this darling little creature. Our home life would be blissful and gratifying. Of course, the normal problems and challenges would arise, but I felt confident that with our background of psychology and child development, my husband and I could handle any problem.

Two years later, I knew differently. I discovered that what had once been an adorable little baby could turn into a biting, tantrum-throwing toddler. She did not respond to the discipline advocated by Dr. Burton White or our college textbooks. Things were no longer blissful, orderly, or quiet. And too often, I was angry or at wit's end. My lofty maternal expectations had been crushed by the reality of motherhood.

Nevertheless, as each year passed, I gathered up the fragments of shattered expectations and formed new ones, only to have them again shattered by reality. I still continue in this process. Perhaps setting expectations that are sometimes beyond the scope of reality is a natural part of motherhood. Perhaps it's only natural that we want to be the best and give the most for those we love so much. And so we strive to be wise disciplinarians, long-suffering nurses, dedicated teachers, cheerful chauffeurs, and patient and loving mothers. In short, we strive to be supermothers.

Living up to lofty personal expectations is difficult, if not impossible. Inevitably, there are times when we fall short. And when we do, we often feel personal dissatisfaction. This personal dissatisfaction can be alleviated, but not by lowering our expectations. We just need to realize that we have not failed if we have not reached our every expectation. In fact, we are far better off falling a little short of a high expectation than we are reaching a low one.

When we do fall short, we simply need to make allowances for "almosts." We can be very successful mothers if we are almost always attentive. We can create a nurturing, supportive home environment if we are almost always loving and patient. Perhaps we aren't patient when a gallon of milk is spilled on our newly waxed floor. And perhaps there are days when we are simply too busy to sit down and read our child a book or play dolls. But if we are generally patient and understanding, and if we frequently spend time with our children, we can feel satisfied and successful in our "almosts."

We can make these allowances for "almosts" because motherhood is not a matter of absolutes. If we have not completely met our expectations, it doesn't mean we have failed. There are too many things to take into consideration to make such a sweeping generalization. It is quite possible to both fall short of and exceed our expectations of motherhood.

One evening as my five-year-old and three-year-old were arguing over who was touched by whom and my six-month-old baby was clinging to my legs crying to be held while I was trying to fix dinner, my husband walked in from work, quickly assessed the situation, and said to me, "Back when we were engaged, did you ever think it would be like this?"

No, I never imagined that I would have a child that complained every night if we didn't have peanut butter and jelly sandwiches for dinner. I never thought that there would be winters when we never had everyone well at one time and that I wouldn't get an uninterrupted night's sleep for years on end. It never dawned on me that there would be times I would feel overwhelmed, exhausted, and inadequate. But neither did I imagine the joy of holding my own baby, the delight of listening to a three-year-old's imaginative play, or the pride of watching my own kindergartner in a school Christmas play. That night in the midst of chaos, I realized that the expectations of motherhood are not always fulfilled, but often they are surpassed.

Distorted Perceptions

Many amusement parks have fun houses full of moving stairs, enormous rolling barrels to walk through, and other paraphernalia that tests balance and dexterity. Also most fun houses have mirrors that distort one's reflection. Some of the mirrors distort the image to tall and thin, others distort it to short and fat, and some distort it to a wavy, rubbery image. However, it doesn't take a fun house mirror to distort one's self-image—the bathroom mirror will do just fine.

According to a survey taken in November of 1980, when most women look into a mirror they see a distorted image: most see a body that is heavier than it actually is. The results of this survey were reported in the *Ogden Standard Examiner:* "Society's obsession with beauty and slimness is distorting self-image in young women. Dissatisfaction with body image was found in 91 percent of the college women surveyed in a recent study described in the November Journal of the American Dietetic Association. Almost 70 percent thought of themselves as overweight, although only 39 percent could be so classified by objective measurement.

"One-fourth of the women were underweight, but less than 10 percent saw themselves that way. And 46 percent wished to be underweight. In all categories—underweight, slightly underweight, normal, slightly overweight, and overweight—63 percent of the women overestimated their size. They perceived themselves to be one category higher than objective assessment indicated."[4]

The same mirror that reflects a distorted physical image also reflects a distorted perception of the importance of being thin. It hasn't always been this way. The classical statues of the goddess Venus, whose very name means beauty, contain more marble than would be used today. More than sixteen hundred years later, the baroque paintings still featured beautiful women of grand proportions. And even in the early 1800s, Jane Austen writes sympathetically about women who are thin and slight of figure. But in the 1920s, the flappers appeared and with them came a new ideal for a perfect figure:

skinny to the point of being boyish. Eventually, the obsession with a boyish figure waned, but thinness had gained a foothold in the standards of beauty, which has not yet been relinquished.

Today, the importance of being thin has grown to almost tyrannical proportions. Many women believe that being average isn't enough. Their ultimate goal is to be underweight. And so billions of dollars are spent on diet books, diet aids, and diet food. Each dollar spent represents personal physical dissatisfaction.

Much of this dissatisfaction is unwarranted. As the previous article later pointed out, fifty-eight percent of the women who were classified in the average weight category, wished to be in a lower weight category. This means that most women—even the underweight and average—are taking the pinch test, joining spas and diet centers, and locking their refrigerators. In short, they create and fuel the multibillion dollar industry of weight loss.

Most of the diet industry's products are accessible to any person. The diet books can be bought at any bookstore. Most diet aids are bought over the counter and diet food fills the freezers of the neighborhood grocery store. They are considered safe, yet each could carry this label: "Warning—the surgeon general has determined than an obsession with being thin and beautiful can be hazardous to your mental health and peace of mind."

The danger of this obsession is not founded on the physical aspects of losing weight or being thin, for many Americans could benefit by losing a few pounds. The danger lies in the underlying premise that a woman's value is based on her appearance.

If a woman accepts this premise, she creates a psychological time bomb. This time bomb must one day explode, for inevitably physical beauty fades and appearances alter. If she has no other basis for personal worth, that too is destroyed in the explosion. And so it becomes all important to hang onto beauty and thinness, which society has deemed a necessary element of beauty. It has become so important that aging starlets have become recluses, hiding their wrinkles and gray hair behind the locked doors of their mansions. It has become so important that women are afraid to grow old.

Recently, I was listening to a talk show where the discussion was beauty pageants. One woman called in and said, "I am a thirty-two-year-old beautiful person. I am in show business. I have a conflict because at this age I am already considering plastic surgery and trying to decide how I will keep up my good looks." This woman had confused beauty with self-worth, and so at age thirty-two, her self-worth was crumbling. She had accepted the premise that a woman's value is based on her appearance.

It is a great tragedy when people feel that because they are not physically attractive, they are worth less than those who are. This tragedy is epitomized in the legend of Cyrano de Bergerac. Cyrano de Bergerac was witty, poetic, courageous, admired, and talented, but he had an enormous nose. He was also in love with a beautiful woman named Roxane. Because of his ugliness, he determined himself unworthy of Roxane and remained silent. He felt his appearance made him undeserving of love.

Cyrano's pain was revealed when he expressed his feelings to his friend, Le Bret. Cyrano said: "Look at me and tell me what hope this protuberance might leave me! I have no illusions. Sometimes, in the blue shadows of evening, I give way to tender feelings. I go into a garden, smelling the fragrance of spring with my poor monstrous nose, and watch a man and a woman strolling together in the moonlight. I think how much I, too, would like to be walking arm in arm with a woman, under the moon. I let myself be carried away, I forget myself—and then I suddenly see the shadow of my profile on the garden wall."[5]

Cyrano denied himself the happiness and love he ardently desired because he had accepted the premise that a person's value is based on his appearance.

This premise is erroneous. Value is not dependent on appearance. Value is separate and apart. In fact, physical beauty and personal value are quite opposite by their very nature. Physical beauty is apparent immediately to every passerby. A woman's individual value unfolds gradually to her friends and close associates as they discover all the unique and endearing facets of her personality. Physical beauty can be enhanced or created through man-made cosmetics or plastic surgery. A person's value is adorned only by intangibles: a listening ear, an understanding heart, and acts of kindness, love, and service. Physical beauty is ephemeral; personal value is eternal.

Christ understood the nature of physical beauty and personal value. He revealed which is more important to God when he instructed Samuel as follows: "Look not on his countenance, or on the height of his stature; because I have refused him: for the LORD seeth not as man seeth; for man looketh on the outward appearance, but the LORD looketh on the heart." (1 Samuel 16:7.) Yet, too often we see only as man seeth. We ignore the heart and give appearance supreme importance. We become obsessed with physical appearances. This obsession consumes our time, energy, and personal satisfaction. In fact, many of the important and fulfilling things of life are slighted or ignored because of our distorted perception of the importance of beauty and thinness.

In 1845, Henry David Thoreau took up residence in the woods at Walden Pond. There he lived for just over two years. He reveals his reason for doing so in his book *Walden*. He says: "I went to the woods because I wished to live deliberately, to front only the essential facts of life, and see if I could not learn what it had to teach, and not, when I came to die, discover that I had not lived. I did not wish to live what was not life, living is so dear. . . . I wanted to live deep and suck out all the marrow of life."[6]

When we become obsessed with beauty and thinness, when much of our mental energy is consumed with thoughts of what to eat, what not to eat, and fears of gaining weight or growing older and less physically beautiful, we are not living life. We are living a shallow semblance of life. We are living a life of distorted perceptions.

To attain personal satisfaction we must begin by eliminating comparative thinking, unrealistic expectations, and distorted perceptions of the importance of physical beauty. But this is only the first step. We must also act assertively to establish the attitudes and habits that foster satisfaction. Two of these attitudes are accepting ourselves unconditionally and being patient during self-improvement.

Unconditional Acceptance

There once was a man who took great pride in his lawn. He meticulously trimmed the shrubberies; he carefully groomed the grass; he weeded out any undesirable elements. One summer, dandelions began to pop up in his lawn. He hoed, he sprayed, and he dug. Still he could not get rid of the dandelions. He consulted gardeners and followed their professional suggestions. The dandelions remained. In desperation he wrote to the Department of Agriculture, listing all the things he tried. He concluded the letter by asking, "What shall I do now?"

Soon his reply came. It read, "We suggest that you learn to love them."[7]

Certain things will never be changed. Short of plastic surgery, there is no correction for a big nose. Nothing can

[handwritten margin note: excellent story of love of acceptance]

make us shorter. Even diets and exercise cannot completely change certain physiological tendencies such as thick ankles or large thighs. These unchangeables are the things we need to learn to love and accept. Doing so unconditionally is paramount to the development of our personal satisfaction.

Unconditional acceptance is something that is easy for many of us, as long as it is for someone else. We fell in love with and married our husbands in spite of any character flaws. We love our children unconditionally. We accept friends whether or not they have big noses or crooked teeth. But do we accept ourselves unconditionally? Do we love ourselves when we have gained five pounds? Do we love ourselves with eyeglasses? Do we love ourselves even though we have big feet or freckles? Or do we object to ourselves because we do not correspond with the current touchstone of beauty?

Joseph Smith once said, "Suppose that Jesus Christ and holy angels should object to us upon frivolous things, what would become of us? We must be merciful to one another, and overlook small things."[8] We need to be merciful to ourselves and accept those things that cannot be changed as part of our God-given uniqueness.

Sometimes we object to ourselves because of our behavior. We go to bed at night and instead of counting sheep, we count the different ways we blew it during the day. "I shouldn't have yelled at Lindsey when she broke the plate. I shouldn't have eaten that second piece of cake. I shouldn't have skipped reading my scriptures." This recounting is generally emotionally charged, so not only do we count our mistakes, but we mentally flog ourselves for these errors. Each stripe lacerates our self-acceptance.

Our self-acceptance and personal satisfaction would be far better off if we followed Emerson's advice. He said, "Finish each day and be done with it. . . . You have done what you could; some blunders and absurdities no doubt crept in; forget them as soon as you can. Tomorrow is a new day; you shall begin it well and serenely."

Such self-acceptance is not synonymous with complacence. Rather it separates personal worth from behavior. It does for us what we do for our children when we tell them, "I love you, but I don't like what you did." In other words, we can disapprove of our behavior, resolve to change it, and still love and accept ourselves.

Self-acceptance encompasses both change and acceptance. If there is something about ourselves that we do not like, we should change it. But this change should not be accompanied by guilt and personal distaste. If the thing we dislike cannot be changed, we should accept it and even learn to love it. This balance of change and acceptance is the key to self-acceptance and the basis for personal contentment.

Patience during Improvement

Most of us realize that in order to become a piano virtuoso, a prima ballerina, a great artist, or an Olympic medalist, it takes dedication, perseverance, and hard work. But these things alone are not enough. It also takes time.

The same is true for us. It takes time to master the art of motherhood. It takes time to become proficient at managing a home. It takes time to master our own selves. And though we are generous in granting years to the aspiring artist to perfect his talent, we begrudgingly allot ourselves a week—maybe two—to become patient with our children, lose 10 pounds, and become completely organized. We strive for perfection, but are impatient in our pursuit. We resemble the man who prayed, "Lord grant me patience, and I want it now!" In order to have personal satisfaction, we need to develop patience for personal improvement.

An important aspect of becoming more patient is making

realistic expectations of the speed at which we will progress. B. F. Skinner, the pioneer of behavioral psychology, records in *Walden Two* the following statement:

"I remember the rage I used to feel when a prediction went awry. I could have shouted at the subjects of my experiments, . . . 'Behave as you ought!' Eventually I realized that the subjects were always right. It was I who was wrong. I had made a bad prediction."[9]

Sometimes we make bad predictions of ourselves, expecting too much too fast. When we don't meet these expectations, we often become impatient with our progress and mentally shout at ourselves, "Behave as you ought!" Adjusting our expectations to correspond to a realistic rate of progress can help us eliminate this personal disappointment and help us become patient with our progress.

Another aspect of becoming patient is understanding success as it relates to improvement. In the Book of Mormon, Jacob decries the Jews for being blind, "which blindness came by looking beyond the mark." (Jacob 4:14.) In our quest for improvement, we often do the same thing. We look beyond the true nature of success and focus on some future, culminating event. Instead of focusing solely on an end result or a distant mark, we need to focus on the process to improvement for it is from the process that we truly derive both success and fulfillment.

Success, more than anything else, is the consistent advancement toward predetermined goals. It is a journey and not a destination. In application, this means that success in parenting is not the day we have mastered patience with our children (for surely by then they have all moved away from home), but success is each time we are patient in a difficult situation. In physical fitness, success is not the day we can run five miles; it is being able to run one mile, then two miles, then three and four miles. Success is not scaling the mountain of personal improvement; success is hiking each switchback that leads up the mountain.

In the same manner, fulfillment should come from the process, not from the final result. This is important for two reasons. First, if we find fulfillment only in final results, we deny ourselves a great deal of joy and fulfillment that comes from the more expansive process. Second, we cannot always control the final result. Forces beyond our control can enter in and alter the final result. If we receive fulfillment from the process, this doesn't matter. Somerset Maugham touched upon this in *Of Human Bondage.* Through the character of Clutton, a struggling painter, he says: "If we force our vision on the world, it calls us great painters; if we don't it ignores us; but *we* are the same. . . . What happens to our work afterwards is unimportant; we have got all that we could out of it while we were doing it."[10]

If we get all we can out of our efforts to improve and succeed, we can be patient with ourselves. This patience is essential for personal satisfaction.

We are not guaranteed personal satisfaction when we enter this life, but we can create it. In order to do so, we must eliminate comparative thinking, unrealistic expectations, and distorted perceptions. We must also accept ourselves unconditionally and be patient with our progress. Doing these things will help us find personal satisfaction.

FINDING SATISFACTION AMIDST FAILURE

*I*n Forbury Park in Reading, England there stands a beautiful statue of a lion. Once a block of stone, the statue is now a masterful representation of the most ferocious beast of the jungle. The muscular legs and body portray the power and strength of the lion. The face captures its majesty. The statue is flawless, except for one thing. The legs are carved in a walking position, with the right front leg and the right back leg both forward and the left front leg and the left back leg both back. But a lion does not walk this way. The sculpture is anatomically incorrect. When the sculptor realized his error, he committed suicide.

Failure can be devastating. It can break a woman's spirit. It can taunt and torment her. It can humiliate her and shatter her dreams and confidence. In essence, it can utterly destroy her personal satisfaction. But this destructive power comes not from failure itself, but rather from how a person responds to failure. By learning positive approaches to failure, we can learn how to fail and still keep our personal satisfaction intact.

Accepting Failure

The time when a baby learns to walk is an exciting time for

both parents and baby. Parents delight in watching their child's short legs hesitantly take a step while his arms are poised for balance. He takes a step, then tumbles. He takes two steps and tumbles again. Each little success is followed by failure. Parents instinctively minimize the failures and loudly applaud the successful attempts. When junior does fail, mom or dad directly picks him up and sets him on his feet to try again. And so it continues: junior walking and falling, and mom and dad clapping and helping.

As adults, we have long since mastered the skills of walking, talking, eating, and drinking, skills that seem easy to us but are monumental to a baby. We have outgrown the need for a steadying hand to help us walk and a loving parent to fasten our buttons and tie our shoes. But we have not outgrown the process of learning and achievement in which success and failure are inseparably connected. Like a baby learning to walk, we take a few steps toward our goal, and then we stumble. We take a few more steps, and then we stumble again. This process is still the same as it was when we were learning to walk. The only thing that has changed is the nature of the tasks we seek to master.

But somewhere in our growing up, we have forgotten that failing is a part of succeeding. We view failure as the antithesis of success. Such is not the case. As the Reverend William E. Phifer, Jr., has said, "Do you know how to fail? If you do, then you will know also the secret of succeeding, for the two are forever locked together."[1] The reason success and failure are so closely intertwined is because they are both products of the same process.

An example of this is Thomas Edison. In 1876 he set up a laboratory where he could devote all his time and energy to inventing things. Before moving into this laboratory, he promised that he would turn out a minor invention every ten days and a major invention every six months. Soon, he had forty different projects he was working on and was applying for as many as four hundred patents a year. Not every one of those inventions were successful. Some were inoperable and some had no mass appeal. But the same creative thought that produced the unsuccessful inventions also produced the inventions that revolutionized the nineteenth century. The thought process was the same.

As it was for Thomas Edison, so it is for us. Success and failure are the products of the same process. Whether we paint a beautiful portrait or a mediocre one, we go through the same process. Whether we bowl a strike or a gutter ball, we must take the same steps, lift our arm, and roll the ball. The process is the same.

One evening I was making blueberry muffins for our dinner. As it was almost dinnertime, I hurriedly broke two eggs into the mixer bowl and turned on the mixer. I added the sugar, the milk, the flour, and the salt. I then added two tablespoons of what I thought was baking powder. The bowl turned around on the mixer base and the white powdery substance slowly disappeared into the lumpy batter. As I turned to put the ingredients back into my cupboard, I realized I had used baking soda instead of baking powder. Unsure of what the outcome might be, I finished the muffins, hoping there wouldn't be much difference. When I took the muffins from the oven, they looked beautiful and smelled wonderful. I was encouraged, until I sampled one. They were the most bitter things I had ever tasted.

The process for making delicious muffins was the same as for making bitter ones. I beat the eggs, sugar, and flour in exactly the same way. I folded in the blueberries and cooked them the same way. Bitter blueberry muffins and delicious blueberry muffins both came from the same process. There was only one variable, and that variable transformed success into failure. It is the same for most successes and failures.

They are not diametrically opposed. They are different results of the same process.

Another notion most of us have accepted, while growing from child to adult, is that failing at something makes us a failure as a person. But failing does not mean we are inept or incapable. It does not indicate we have inferior abilities and talents. What it does indicate is that we have attempted to succeed.

While I was playing on our ward's softball team, my husband frequently came to our games to give me moral support, encouragement, and advice. On one occasion he was giving me some pointers on running the bases.

"What you need to do," he said, "is to watch the other team's players. Watch how far and how accurately they throw the ball. If you know the center fielder has a poor arm, when a ball is hit to center field you can take two bases without stopping to look around. Of course, sometimes you will get out. But for myself, I would rather die going to third than stand at second."

So it is with all kinds of success. In attempting to succeed, we must also risk failure. But we are better off failing while attempting to improve and grow than we are if we succeed at doing nothing. General George B. McClellan, one of Abraham Lincoln's generals in the Civil War, was so fearful of making mistakes and failing as the leader of the Northern forces, that he conducted a waiting campaign. In essence, he stood safely on second. Exasperated with this inactivity, Lincoln sent him this message:

"My dear McClellan: If you don't want to use the army I should like to borrow it for a while.

Yours respectfully,
A. Lincoln."[2]

What Lincoln wanted was a general who would take charge of

the situation and aggressively take the offensive, even though it meant taking a risk. When he found this kind of a general in Ulysses S. Grant, the tide of the war turned.

The more frequently we attempt to succeed, the greater the risk of failing becomes—but the opportunity for success also increases. In 1979, Carl Yastrzemski of the Boston Red Sox became the fifteenth player in baseball history to have three thousand hits. This event received a lot of attention from the media. Asked whether all the attention was going to his head, he replied, "I look at it this way: in my career I've been up to bat over ten thousand times. That means I've been unsuccessful at the plate over seven thousand times. That fact alone keeps me from getting a swollen head."[3]

In order to achieve his goal, Carl Yastrzemski risked failing over ten thousand times. Of those ten thousand times, he failed seven thousand times. Had he not attempted to succeed so many times, he would not have failed seven thousand times, but neither would he have achieved a goal that only fourteen other players had ever achieved.

Seeing failure for what it is, an attempt to succeed and a product of the same process that leads to success, gives failure a new perspective. It helps us accept failure without allowing it to damage our self-esteem or our personal satisfaction.

Valuing Progress

The second element in a positive approach to failure is valuing the progress we have made. The story is told of a missionary convention held many years ago where missionaries from all parts of the world were gathered. Each reported the great strides being made in spreading Christianity to the heathens. One missionary had been working with some cannibals in Africa. He, too, boasted of great progress. After he gave his report, he was asked if he had stopped the cannibals from eating human flesh.

"Unfortunately," replied the missionary, "I have not stopped their cannibalism. But we have made great progress. Before they were eating human flesh with their hands. Now they eat with knives and forks."[4]

We need this missionary's appreciation for progress. Progress is one of the few truly accurate rulers we have for measuring success. We cannot compare ourselves with others and come up with an accurate assessment of ourselves. We cannot use the standards of wealth, status, and beauty. These may indicate worldly success, but worldly success is superficial when compared to success of the inner man. But we can compare ourselves today with ourselves of yesterday and a year ago and five years ago. If we have made progress, we are truly successful even if we have failed to reach our goals in their entirety.

Closely related to valuing progress is giving ourselves credit for what we have done. Within the past year, my husband has attempted to teach me the game of golf. I discovered that this game fits the description given it by Arnold Daley: "If you don't take it seriously, it's no fun; if you do take it seriously, it's apt to break your heart."[5] The more serious I became in my desire to improve, the more frustrated I became. Finally, after one particularly short drive during a particularly poor round, my husband clearly read the disgust written all over my face. He took me aside and said, "Amy, give yourself some credit. Look at what you did—you hit the ball. (This was a definite improvement over my first time at the driving range.) It went straight. It's in the fairway. So what if it didn't go very far? Give yourself credit for what you did."

This lesson was an important one for me to learn. It not only helped me with golf, it has helped me appreciate losing only two pounds when I wanted to lose four. It has helped me give myself credit for getting six loads of laundry done even though I didn't get the socks folded. It has helped me value the progress I've made toward a goal, though I didn't reach the goal in its entirety. Most of all, it has helped me maintain personal satisfaction, even in the midst of failure.

Learning from Failure

While a prisoner in Liberty Jail, Joseph Smith received and recorded revelation from the Lord. One verse from that revelation reads as follows:

"If thou shouldst be cast into the pit, or into the hands of murderers, and the sentence of death passed upon thee; if thou be cast into the deep; if the billowing surge conspire against thee; if fierce winds become thine enemy; if the heavens gather blackness, and all the elements combine to hedge up the way; and above all, if the very jaws of hell shall gape open the mouth wide after thee, *know thou, my son, that all these things shall give thee experience, and shall be for thy good.*" (D&C 122:7; italics added.)

This counsel was intended to help Joseph endure the tremendous amount of persecution heaped upon him by his enemies. However, it is equally valuable in helping us deal with failure. In every failure there is something that can give us experience. There is something that will be for our good if we learn from it.

In 1837, Benjamin Disraeli entered the British political arena. His road to political success had been fraught with failure. Four different times, he had unsuccessfully sought a seat in parliament. Before that, he had failed repeatedly in business and finance. He had lost a substantial amount of money through speculation in South American mining, incurring a debt that stayed with him well past middle age. He had launched a daily newspaper that was a complete failure. And he had produced an anonymous satirical novel that was soon identified as his and for which he was sharply criticized.

Finally, with his election to parliament, it looked as if the tide of failure had turned. But when he appeared in the House of Commons for his maiden speech, he was a dismal failure. His dress was foppish and ostentatious, his manner affected, and his speech saturated with elaborate metaphors. Because of his pretense and self-aggrandizement, he cut a ridiculous figure. Because of his verbosity, his speech was a failure. In fact, his failure was so complete that he was howled down. The laughter and jeers were so clamorous that he had to shout his final words just to be heard. In spite of this, his closing words revealed an unabashed spirit of determination. He shouted, "I will sit down now, but the time will come when you will hear me."[6]

Disraeli heeded the lesson of experience and altered his manner and style of speaking until he eventually became a most eloquent and respected speaker. He commanded the attention of kings, queens, and parliaments, and he twice rose to the summit of British politics as the country's prime minister.

Failure, as evidenced by Disraeli, is not easy, but it can be valuable. It can offer us experience and be for our good if we approach it positively. As Fred Adler, one of the United State's premier venture capitalists, has said, "If you've analyzed how and why you've failed, and how you would handle it in the future, then [failure] is a positive experience."[7]

Learning to Drop Back and Punt

We can learn another positive approach to failure by looking at the game of football. A football team is given four chances to achieve the goal of gaining ten yards. If it fails to reach this goal, it has three options. The most frequently taken option is kicking, or punting, the football to their opposition. Because football players know they will not always reach their goal, they practice this option over and over. Likewise, we should realize there will be times when we won't reach a goal. We, too, should know how to implement an alternative plan when necessary. We should be able to drop back and punt.

Learning to drop back and punt helps us deal positively with failure; it transforms failure from a final judgment into a signal to explore other options. And in exploring other options, we often find success in unexpected ways.

There was once a young Frenchman whose heartfelt ambition was to become a pilot. Because he seriously hurt his arm in an accident, he was prohibited from flying. He "dropped back and punted," and Jacques Cousteau became a pilot of the ocean. In this profession he has been eminently successful, having written several books and produced numerous films concerning the ocean. He invented the Aqualung diving apparatus and a process for filming television underwater. He also founded or headed many research groups.

Walt Disney was another man who, when faced with an apparent failure, dropped back and punted. In the early days of his career, he and his partner were cheated by a New York film distributor. Destitute and disheartened, he pursued another option and went to Los Angeles to join his brother Roy. There they began working on cartoons that lead to creation of Mickey Mouse.

When faced with obstacles and barriers that prohibit us from reaching our goals, we too can drop back and punt. Like Disney and Cousteau, we might find unprecedented success. If we do not, we have still successfully lessened the sting of failure by responding to it assertively and positively.

Failure can be devastating. It can torment us, humiliate us, and overwhelm us. Most of all, it can destroy our personal satisfaction unless we learn a positive approach that includes accepting failure, valuing progress, learning from failure, and dropping back to punt.

DEFINING PURPOSE AND DIRECTION

*D*wight Morrow, a distinguished ambassador to Mexico in the 1920s, was once traveling on a train. When it came time to hand the conductor his ticket, Mr. Morrow could not find it. He searched his pockets and fumbled through his briefcase, but still could not find his ticket. The more he searched, the more uncomfortable he became. The conductor recognized him and said, "Don't worry, Mr. Morrow, I'm certain you have your ticket. When you find it, mail it to the company."

"Worry be hanged," Mr. Morrow exploded. "If I don't find the ticket, I won't know where I'm going!"[1]

Many people are like Dwight Morrow. They simply do not know where they are going. They have not identified the purpose or the direction of their lives. Yet a definite purpose and direction is one of the most powerful forces and most beneficial aids a person can have.

It is especially important for a woman who is a full-time mother and homemaker to have a well-defined purpose and direction, because she may find herself with few external forces that dictate what her purpose or direction should be. No manager or supervisor imposes his standards or policies. No organization dictates that she must meet certain quotas or perform at a certain level. Rather, her purpose and direction are self-determined. She decides how her life will be ordered and what she will accomplish. This direction comes from within.

Determining Your Life's Purpose

We live in a society where the traditional family unit (the husband works and the wife is a full-time homemaker) is now a minority. The United States Labor Department reported that as of the end of 1984, three-fifths of the nation's married women with children under eighteen were working. And of married women with children one year old or younger, nearly half are in the labor force. In 1970 this same statistic was twenty-four percent. With this sociological change has also come a change in attitudes about women and their roles.

Recently my husband came home from work and told me a friend had stopped by to visit him at work. This friend was a career saleswoman who had married a year previously. As she shared with him some of her trials and joys of her first year of marriage, she interjected, "We would like to have a baby, but I'm afraid I'd be ashamed to say I was just a mother."

Such is the attitude of many. In today's society, it is more socially acceptable to be a company executive than it is to be a mother. It is more socially acceptable for a woman to travel with her job than it is to stay home with her children. It is more socially acceptable for a woman to reach her full potential by pursuing a career than it is to spend her life helping her children reach their full potential.

Because of this lack of support from society, a woman who has chosen the career of mother and homemaker needs to have an internal conviction that her work is important, and that her life as a mother and homemaker has a definite and worthwhile purpose. This personal conviction can be obtained through direct, personal revelation from God. From him, the divine purpose of our lives can be unfolded, and we can know without a doubt where we should direct our energies and what should be the focus of our lives.

Obtaining this personal conviction begins with defining the purpose of your life. This is more than choosing a purpose as randomly as college freshmen choose a major. A life's purpose needs to be carefully considered, because Satan has offered many counterfeit purposes that seem attractive and worthwhile by the world's standards. Just as the most poisonous mushrooms closely resemble the prized, edible ones, the most prized purposes of life can easily be confused with ones that are eventually revealed to be bitter and sometimes lethal counterfeits.

Some of the pain resulting from a poorly chosen life's purpose can be felt by a glimpse into literature. In the summer of 1816, Mary Shelley and her husband Percy Bysshe Shelley visited Switzerland and became neighbors to Lord Byron. A wet summer afforded these literary giants of English romanticism many chances to join together, read, and discuss ideas. During this summer, they discovered a book of German ghost stories, which they read aloud. Upon finishing them, Lord Byron declared, "We will each write a ghost story."

Mary Shelley industriously applied herself to the task and created the tale of a young man who became obsessed with the idea of instilling life into an inanimate creation. For two years, all of this man's time, thought, and energy were focused to this end. Finally, on a dreary November night, this man's dream was realized. However, he did not feel joy and elation on this momentous occasion. The following words scribbled in his journal convey the feelings of his heart and soul:

"I had worked hard for nearly two years, for the sole purpose of infusing life into an inanimate body. For this I had deprived myself of rest and health. I had desired it with an ardour that far exceeded moderation; but now that I had finished, the beauty of the dream vanished, and breathless horror and disgust filled my heart."[2]

This horror never subsided. Indeed, it augmented daily, poisoning his thoughts, his dreams, and his happiness. Eventually, it destroyed Monsieur Frankenstein, the creator of a monster.

We must carefully choose our life's purpose or we may one day discover we have spent our entire lifetime pursuing something that does not bring us happiness. Unlike Monsieur Frankenstein, we will probably not see our goal personified— walking, breathing, and destroying life. Nonetheless, its effects will be just as real, perhaps destroying our family life, our happiness, and our eternal rewards.

Such disastrous mistakes can be avoided by taking time to consider such questions as, "What things give me the greatest and longest lasting happiness?" "What am I here on this earth to do?" and "What is it that would give me the greatest joy and pride when accounting for my life?"

We can take the answers to these questions and formulate a purpose for our life. When we have done this, we need to prayerfully seek a confirmation of that purpose. Through prayer, we can know without a doubt what should be the focus of our lives and subsequently how we should direct our energies.

However, chances are that this purpose will not be revealed in a panoramic scene after an evening prayer. Instead, it will probably begin with a warm feeling of peace given by the Holy Ghost. The more specific purposes of our life will unfold decision by decision as we prayerfully and faithfully seek spiritual guidance.

When we have formulated a purpose for our life and have obtained a confirmation of it, we should write it down. Writing it down has a way of transforming it from a desire or wish to a real goal. It also strengthens our commitment to that purpose and helps to hone it to a precise purpose.

Just as there are many facets of life, there can be many facets to the purpose of life. For instance, the following could all be a part of our life's purpose: working out our own salvation, developing our own talents, being an excellent and committed mother, building a relationship with our spouse that will last an eternity.

When you have carefully chosen your life's purpose, which has been confirmed through prayer and written down, you are ready to move on to directing your life to that purpose.

Giving Your Life Direction

One Sunday, as soon as we arrived home from church, our five-year-old daughter ran outside to the backyard. In just a moment, she came in carrying a small plastic container. Curious as to what she was doing, I looked into her container and saw six wrinkly raisins. Bubbling over with excitement, she said, "Look, Mom, I made grapes."

After chatting with her for a few moments, I realized she had mixed up the process of turning grapes into raisins. She started with the end result (the raisins) and had attempted to work backwards (to dry them out to turn them into grapes).

At first, I regarded the incident as simply another insertion in my notebook of cute things the kids say. However, I soon realized that the concept of working backwards can be a very valuable one—except when trying to make grapes. Working backwards can be especially valuable in planning our activities, and lives.

Often as homemakers, we are busy every minute of the day. We can be efficient, organized, and successful at accomplishing everything on our lists and yet still not be moving toward the ultimate purpose of our life. The problem is not a lack of motivation or organization; we are simply working on a day-to-day or week-to-week basis. Our vision is limited to the here and now and to the near future. Working backwards, starting from eternity and working back to today, solves this. It ensures that our busy days are leading us to where we ultimately want to be.

Each step in planning backwards is made with consideration given to the previous goal. So after first prayerfully and carefully choosing a life's purpose, the next step is to choose lifetime goals that correspond to the purpose we've chosen. These lifetime goals should be specific and concrete. For instance, from the ultimate purpose of working out your own salvation, you could derive such lifetime goals as magnifying your church callings, reading one of the standard works each year, living the Word of Wisdom, and learning about the life of each of the latter-day prophets.

If you want to develop your talents, you could include such goals as being well read in the literary classics, developing your talent of painting, establishing a lifelong exercise program to maintain fitness, or obtaining a college degree.

In the same manner, lifetime goals that pertain to mothering should be determined. Not only should you set goals concerning the kind of mother you want to be, but you should also decide what concepts you want to teach your children and what skills and abilities you want them to have by the time they are adults. For instance, you might decide that you want your children to have a testimony of the truthfulness of the gospel, to be responsible, to understand how to earn and manage money, to have a love for knowledge, to be decisive, and to always feel love, security, and acceptance in your family.

Such specific lifetime goals in parenting are essential. Without them, teaching and learning still take place, but they are more haphazard, and are usually prompted by last Sunday's Relief Society lesson, a good article on parenting, or what seems needful at the time. Specific goals of exactly which principles you want your children to learn define what learning should take place and why. They give order and purpose to the things we teach our children and help us become aware of teaching opportunities we might otherwise have passed by.

Lifetime parenting goals are also valuable in giving meaning and purpose to the daily tasks that consume so much of a mother's time. With the things we want to teach our children laid out before us, new importance is given to the hours we spend cradling babies, helping a child learn his alphabet, teaching a child how to make his bed, or bandaging the tiny though excruciatingly painful wounds of a toddler. We are establishing the environment of love when we cradle a baby and bandage wounds. We are teaching a child to desire knowledge when teaching him the alphabet. And we are planting the seeds of responsibility while teaching a child to make his bed.

These are small things, but when considered from the vantage point of what we want to accomplish in life, we can see they are the foundation of a great work. They are, as the Doctrine and Covenants states, the small things from which proceedeth that which is great. (See D&C 64:33.)

When we know what we are ultimately trying to accomplish, each day of our life has meaning and importance, regardless of how trivial and routine the everyday tasks seem. In *The Wisdom of the Sands,* Antoine de Saint-Exupery writes of the meaning that is given to common tasks when there is a purpose to them. He writes:

"Joyful is swimming when it brings you nearer a shore slowly emerging from the sea. And joyful the creak of the pulley, bringing you the water for which you thirst. . . . What do you become within yourself if you turn the handle merely so as to hear the pulley, or sew the mantle merely for the mantle's sake . . . ? All these things are soon exhausted, for they have nothing to give you."[3]

And so it is for us. Each day of our life and each task of the day can be fraught with meaning when we have defined our lifetime goals.

The next step in planning backwards is planning yearly goals. This, too, is done in consideration of the previous goals. With your lifetime goals in front of you, determine what you would like to do in the next twelve months that will bring you closer to your lifetime goals. For example, under the lifetime goal of magnifying your church calling, you might decide that for the next year you will have a hundred percent visiting teaching each month or do a special something with one of your Primary students each month. From the lifetime goal of reading one of the standard works each year, you might set the yearly goal to read the Book of Mormon. From the lifetime goal of learning about each of the latter-day prophets, you might set the yearly goal of reading three books about Brigham Young.

The same kind of selection would be done for your personal and parenting lifetime goals. You do not need to have a yearly goal derived from each lifetime goal. For instance, if you now have three preschool children, you may want to wait a few years before working on your lifetime goal of obtaining a college degree.

Yearly goals can be chosen at any time, but a logical time to do it is at the beginning of the year when the spirit of resolutions and new beginnings is strong. However, planning the year's goals is different from setting New Year's resolutions. So often people begin the year with grandiose plans for eradicating every vice from their lives and starting twenty-three personal improvement programs. Understandably, within a few weeks or a month at most, their good intentions have waned and their improvement programs have been tossed aside, with a twinge of guilt, until next year. On the other hand, planning for the next year does not mean tackling every goal in the next two weeks. Rather, these goals are to be interspersed throughout the year as we are ready for them. This gradual introduction of our yearly goals takes place as we plan each month.

As with all the other steps in planning backwards, monthly goals are planned in consideration of the previous goals. From your yearly goal plan, you can decide which goals you would like to work on for the next month. Remember, this is a selection process; you do not need to work on all of your goals each month.

From your yearly goal of doing something special with one of your Primary students each month, you could plan to take a certain student out for an ice cream cone and have twenty minutes with her on a one-on-one basis to talk with her about her interests. From the goal of reading the Book of Mormon, you could decide to read First Nephi. From the goal of learning about the latter-day prophets, you could plan on reading fifty pages from *The Discourses of Brigham Young.* Again, this process is repeated with your other yearly goals.

Monthly goals are then reduced to weekly goals. From your monthly goal of taking a certain Primary student out for an ice cream cone and personal time, you could decide to do this on a specific day of the week. From your monthly goal to read First Nephi, you could decide to read First Nephi chapters one through six. From your monthly goal to read fifty pages from *The Discourses of Brigham Young,* you could decide to read fifteen pages.

Daily planning takes only a few minutes and will be elaborated on a little later.

The whole system of planning backwards is like a Russian

nesting doll. Just as each doll opens up to reveal a smaller doll, each step in planning backwards reveals a more specific and shorter range goal. The smallest nesting doll is so tiny that it is hard to believe it is the same kind as the beautiful, more ornate larger dolls. Comparatively, daily and weekly goals are so simple, it's hard to believe they are a part of the more ambitious lifetime goals. Then when the nesting doll is reassembled, each little doll fits snugly into the larger one until the doll is again in one piece. And as time progresses, each goal naturally leads to the next one until one day you have accomplished your lifetime goals and life's purpose.

Planning Your Life

Much of the success of planning backwards is dependent on keeping your goals before you. Doing so is not complicated or difficult; it simply requires about one hour a week and a notebook. Getting a notebook should be no problem at all. Any loose-leaf notebook will do. With it, you also need dividers and lined paper.

First, divide your notebook into four sections: Life's Purpose, Lifetime Goals, Yearly Goals, and Monthly Goals. Record your different level of goals on a different sheet of paper and file it behind the appropriate divider.

Finding an uninterrupted hour each week may prove difficult for many mothers. Uninterrupted hours are hard to find, but they can be made. It might require enlisting the aid of your husband. If he is less than enthusiastic at the prospect, remind him that it's not just an hour spent, it's an hour invested. That one hour of planning yields greater productivity for the next week, month, and year. It also has the magical power of transforming a frazzled housewife into a loving wife and mother with fresh commitment. Linda Eyre, in her book *A Joyful Mother of Children,* describes the weekly hour of planning as "the key to your success for the week" and without it she finds that she is "unorganized and irritable." She reports, "Nothing you do during the week is more important than that hour of concentrated planning."[4]

If your husband is unable to provide this hour, find some way to provide it for yourself, even if it means getting up early, going to bed late, or putting your oldest child in charge of the family. This hour is critical.

Sunday is an excellent day for the weekly goal planning session. Personal planning and study is a perfect Sunday activity. Many husbands are home and therefore can help provide you with an uninterrupted hour. In addition, you will have everything planned and ready to go when the Monday morning alarm rings.

So while your husband wrestles with, reads to, or naps with the kids, isolate yourself. Lock the door and let it be known you open it only for emergencies. Lost shoes, sibling fights, telephone calls, and snack time do not constitute emergencies.

If you desire, begin with prayer. Next, read your life's purpose. Read your lifetime goals. Read your yearly goals. Read your monthly goals. And from your monthly goals, plan your weekly goals.

In planning my weekly goals, I divide the top three inches of the paper into four columns. The first column is for my personal goals. The second is for my spiritual goals. The third is for my family-oriented goals. The fourth is for my weekly tasks and house-related responsibilities.

Linda Eyre suggests assigning symbols to the different categories of goals.[5] I have found this valuable in that the categories are recognizable at a glance. My personal goals I note with a square. I note my spiritual goals with a triangle for it points upward. My family goals are assigned a circle for it represents our family circle and my goals regarding the necessities of my world (my weekly tasks and house-related responsibilities) are assigned a symbol of the world—a diamond.

In my columns headed with a square, triangle, circle, and diamond, I write my goals for the week in their appropriate columns. Some of the goals directly reflect my monthly goals. Others are simply the things I need to do that week, like "get a sitter for Saturday, mend Lindsey's dress, and buy material for pumpkin costume." With these necessities and my goals listed across the top part of the paper, it is easy to plan what I need to do the next day. It is also easy to quickly review them every evening and plan for the following day. These daily things are written on the bottom part of the paper; I also use the back of the paper if necessary. A few minutes is all that is usually necessary for daily planning. When I'm finished organizing my week, I place the paper listing my weekly and daily goals in the front of my notebook where it is easily accessible.

Each week, a planning session should include reading your life's purpose, lifetime goals, yearly goals, and monthly goals. After reading these, you can review your past week and then plan your next week according to your monthly goals.

On the first Sunday of each month, you can also review your last month's goals, evaluate your success, and set goals for the following month according to your yearly goals. With the new month planned, you can then plan your week.

Once a year, your planning session will probably take more than an hour while you review your past year's goals, evaluate your successes, review your life goals, and set corresponding yearly goals for the next year.

The process is not complicated and takes relatively little time. Yet, it directs each day toward eternity. It keeps our goals in focus and provides logical, attainable steps to reaching long-range goals. Not only does it direct each day toward eternity, it brings eternity into each day.

Seeing eternity in each day is not always easy amidst dishwashers that must always be unloaded, toys that seem to reproduce faster than rabbits, and piles of laundry that if left for a week would rival the size of Mount Everest. It takes stopping at least once a week to review our goals so that each day leads us to eternity. Without this time for planning and review, it's easy to get bogged down in the daily chores. When we are bogged down in daily chores, all we see are jobs to do and tasks to perform. We do not see what is essential, for as de Saint-Exupery wrote in *The Little Prince:* "That which is essential is invisible to the eye."

I understood the impact of this statement one day when I took my daughter to get an ice cream cone. As we were sitting in the store eating our ice cream, two high school students came in, ordered their ice cream, and sat down near us. Since the store was small and we were the only other patrons at the time, their conversation seemed to fill the room. I listened as they talked about the boredom and futility of school and how they passed a class by copying another student's answers during a test. I thought this was very sad, for they had *a* result—a grade—but they did not have *the* result—knowledge. They had overlooked the essential because it was invisible to the eye.

Just as I was feeling both compassionate and endowed with superior wisdom, I realized how often I lose sight of the essential because it is invisible to the eye. I reflected back to the previous morning when I felt swamped with tasks. No matter how many things I cleaned up, everything seemed to be untidy. It didn't take long until I had shifted into my I-want-no-nonsense voice and was shouting orders like a drill sergeant. We got the house cleaned, but it was at the expense of the peace and harmony of our family.

After my rampage, I had a result (a clean, orderly house), but I did not have the essential result (a happy family). The whole purpose of a clean, orderly house is so my family and I can function in a happy, peaceful, and orderly manner. I had forgotten this in my pursuit of the visible, the less essential result. I did not need to sacrifice a clean house, but I did need to keep the essential foremost in my mind.

By setting a life's purpose and directing our efforts to that purpose by setting lifetime, yearly, monthly, and daily goals, we can take control of our life and our time. The things that we do with our time are not haphazard or directed solely by the necessity of the moment, but they lead us to our life's purpose. When we adequately plan, even the acts that may seem mundane or trivial gain significance, for we see them for what they really are: small acts from which proceeds that which is great. In essence, a purpose and direction brings eternity into the moment.

ACHIEVING EXCELLENCE AND SELF-FULFILLMENT

*A*n Englishman, an Irishman, and an American were flying over the Sahara Desert. As they looked down upon the vast expanse stretching below them, the Englishman muttered, "A beastly place."

The Irishman added, "The devil's home."

Then the American voiced his opinion, "What a parking lot!"[1]

Today the home is much like the Sahara Desert. Many people look at it and consider it "a beastly place" for a woman to spend her life and career. They see it as a place of drudgery and mundane tasks suited only for the unambitious. Others see it as "the devil's home," full of squalling kids with dirty faces and dirty diapers. But a few, like the American, look at the home and see opportunity. With profound insight, they see that what may appear to some as a vast desert is actually an oasis replete with opportunities and possibilities for growth, fulfillment, and satisfaction.

Those with this insight see that a woman who is a full-time mother and homemaker is indeed a career woman with tremendous influence and grave responsibilities with consequences that span eternity. Those who lack this insight see the full-time mother and homemaker as a woman without a career. Nothing could be farther from the truth. A mother and homemaker is actually an entrepreneur of the highest order.

In 1983, *Success Magazine* published *Goal-Setting Guide, A Blueprint for Personal Achievement.* (This guide is available through Success Unlimited in Chicago.) In it, they listed seven characteristics a person should have in order to be a successful entrepreneur. They are as follows:

Physical stamina. You can work for long periods of time without exhausting yourself. You are able to adjust to irregular hours of work and sleep.

Responsibility. You have a special flair for taking charge of any situation. Being at the helm and handling different types of problems is very gratifying to you.

High learning curve. You are able to grasp new ideas and tasks quickly.

Commitment. When you begin a project, you work rapidly toward its completion without becoming bored.

Intuition. You are able to arrive at sound decisions quickly.

Delegation of authority. You recognize potential in others about you, and are confident enough to enlist their talents by assigning them to specific tasks.

Risk taking. You are confident enough to take chances because you know how to meet challenges and master them.[2]

Consider how well a homemaker and mother fills these requirements:

Physical stamina. She must work for long periods of time, often starting at 6:00 A.M. and ending at 10:00 or 11:00 P.M. Even then, she is still on call for the next eight hours. She frequently is required to adjust to irregular hours of work and sleep, especially when there is a new baby or a sick child.

Responsibility. She must take care of many types of

problems, from rushing a child to the emergency room or doctor's office for stitches to soothing a child's emotional wounds of loneliness or exclusion; from dealing with equipment failures like an overflowing washing machine to catering for a business dinner—and sometimes these occur all at once.

High learning curve. She must grasp new ideas and skills in childrearing at least yearly (if not monthly or even daily) as children emerge from one developmental stage to another.

Commitment. She is committed to her work because the consequences of her work are eternal.

Intuition. She must quickly arrive at sound buying decisions, sound refereeing decisions and judgment calls, and sound financial planning.

Delegation of authority. She spends considerable energy assigning her children specific tasks, such as making a bed, picking up toys, and washing dishes. She teaches them how to perform those tasks, and gradually withdraws supervision until the task can be performed independently.

Risk taking. She must take chances and risks, especially as she allows her protégés independence in their own decision-making and value choices.

After reading such a specific description, who can dispute that a mother and homemaker is an entrepreneur? And as an entrepreneur, she is indeed a career woman.

The homemaker, like all career women, can derive great personal fulfillment from her career. But as in other careers, it does not just happen. Personal fulfillment depends upon our commitment to personal excellence and upon the degree to which we live up to our standard of excellence.

To bring us closer to our ideal of excellence, we can adapt many of the same principles of success that are beneficial for the business world. Four of these principles especially suitable for adaptation are solution-oriented problem solving, effectiveness versus efficiency, wise investment of time, and true professionalism.

Solution-Oriented Problem Solving

In the business world, a manager's effectiveness is based on his ability to solve problems. The ability to effectively and creatively solve problems is just as valuable for career homemakers who constantly deal with problems of all different sizes and intensities.

One evening, not too long ago, my husband sensed things were not quite right and asked me what was wrong. Within minutes I tearfully recounted a day full of problems, ending with, "I just feel so overwhelmed. There's so much to do!"

He asked, "What can I do to help?"

I wasn't sure. So many of the problems were simply the trials and challenges of motherhood, things like a sick baby that wants to be held all day and the squabbling of siblings engaged in a battle for their toys, the TV, or the trampoline. When these challenges were compounded by a gallon of milk spilled on a newly mopped floor, a batch of homemade rolls that were flat because the yeast had died, and the overall feeling of too much to do and not enough time to do it in, it became too much. And yet, I couldn't isolate anything specific my husband could do to help. The problems were ones that surfaced and demanded attention during the day. The one need I could identify was the need for sympathy and understanding. But I didn't get it, at least not very much of it. Instead, I got solutions.

"So you feel overwhelmed," continued my husband. "What can you do about it? Who could watch the kids one day a week so that you could get out of the house? Do you want someone to come in and help clean the house? Just tell me what you want and let's do it."

His underlying message emphasized another fundamental

of business—results. He wouldn't dwell on the problem or let me dwell on it. Rather, he focused on the desired result of relieving some of the demands on my time and the stress I felt. He was in essence telling me, "Don't spend time feeling sorry for yourself about a problem. Let's just do what we need to to eliminate the problem." While he was not willing to give me sympathy, he was willing to help in whatever way he could to eliminate the problem.

A few weeks later when I again felt overwhelmed with too much to do, I got even less sympathy. "Amy," said my husband a little exasperated, "there's no reason why you have to feel this way. I told you you can hire a babysitter and cleaning help. Take Wednesday for your day off and get away from everything. Eliminate the problem before it happens."

I eventually learned a valuable lesson from my husband and his businesslike approach to problems. I learned the best way to solve a problem is to approach it from a solution-oriented point of view. It saves time, reduces wear and tear on emotions, and gets the results. I had been relying on understanding and appreciation to carry me through difficult periods. Sympathy and understanding are important, but they don't prevent the problems from recurring. Solution-oriented problem solving does.

In *The One Minute Manager,* Kenneth Blanchard and Spencer Johnson advocate solution-oriented problem solving and suggest three steps to help employ it. The first step is to identify the problem in tangible concrete terms. What is it exactly that is causing the problem? For instance, "My kids are driving me crazy" is too vague. Something like "John teases Jason several times a day, Mary isn't picking up her toys, and everyone is irritable at dinnertime" is a far more concrete description of problems.

The next step is to define what behavior you would like to have happen. For instance, "I would like John to be kind to

Jason, Mary to pick up her toys, and for no one to complain about what we are having for dinner or whine that he is starving to death while I fix dinner." Blanchard and Johnson explain why this is a necessary step. They write: "If you can't tell me what you'd like to be happening, you don't have a problem yet. You're just complaining. A problem only exists if there is a difference between what is actually happening and what you desire to be happening."

The third step is determining what needs to be done to get from the problem to the desired result or behavior.[3] Often, these steps become apparent just by defining the problem and the desired behavior or results. For instance, by determining that you don't want kids complaining about their unremitting hunger pangs, it becomes apparent that a plausible solution is to give them a substantial snack a few hours before dinner, which will help tide them over.

Sometimes, the steps are not so apparent. At these times, you might want to consider creative thinking. "Creative thinking," says author Roger von Oech, "requires an attitude or outlook which allows you to search for ideas and manipulate your knowledge and experience. With this outlook, you . . . use crazy, foolish, and impractical ideas as stepping stones to practical new ideas."

One way to do this, he says, is to play the game of "What if ?" This game consists of asking yourself, "What if . . . ?" and then finishing the question with a statement that is contrary to the facts. The answer can be improbable, impossible, or highly imaginative. Some examples are "What if I could travel through time?" "What if the sun always shined night and day?" and "What if money grew in gardens?"

"What-ifing" is fun, but it is also valuable. It was this type of questioning that lead Albert Einstein to some of his early relativity concepts. "What-if" questions can also be valuable in directing us to previously unheard of solutions to our problems. One notable example of this happened in a city in the Netherlands, which had a problem with litter. After trying such things as doubling the littering fine and increasing the number of litter agents—neither of which were successful—someone suggested, "What if our trash cans paid people money when they put their trash in?" This question was too impractical to implement, for if they did what was suggested the city would go bankrupt. But this question did lead to a unique and successful solution: electronic trash cans with tape recorders that would play a joke when trash was deposited.[4]

In the same vein, "what-ifing" can be very valuable in helping us determine solutions to problems we encounter as homemakers. The answers to our "what-if" questions might immediately bring to mind a solution, or they may stimulate our thoughts to another answer. Take for instance the example of the mother who was fed up with fighting children, scattered toys, and dinnertime complaints. The mother could ask herself the following question:

"What if every time Jason teased Johnny, a giant hand came down from the sky and took his tongue out?" This is definitely imaginative and improbable. It does not immediately suggest a solution, but it does lead to another "what-if" question: "What if every time Jason teased Johnny, Jason couldn't talk?" This question, though still physically impossible, has possibilities that can be refined by another question.

"What if every time Jason teased Johnny, no one in the family would talk to Jason for ten minutes?" Taking into account the personality of Jason, this might be a very plausible solution for Jason's teasing. Note that this solution was not immediately apparent from the first "what-if" question, but resulted from a series of "what-ifs."

Another avenue of creative thinking is lateral thinking. Like "what-ifing," lateral thinking implies approaching a problem from a different angle. In his book *The Discovery of Joy,* Richard Eyre describes lateral thinking as "working by faith and by thought rather than by physical force. It is a halfback bouncing along the defensive line running laterally, looking for daylight, rather than a fullback, lowering his head and plowing right into the opposition. It is walking around to the back door instead of trying to knock down the locked front door."[5]

From a mother's viewpoint, lateral thinking is coercing a toddler to exchange a valuable heirloom for a shiny rattle instead of taking the heirloom by force and perchance damaging it. It is motivating a child to feed the garbage gobbler instead of nagging him to do his vacuuming chores. It is taking a child on a treasure hunt for moo juice (milk), golden spears (carrots), and miniature trees (broccoli) instead of dragging him to the grocery store. It is solving an argument using the wisdom of Solomon, instead of just sending the kids to their room. In short, it is solving a problem creatively, from a new angle when old solutions and old angles don't work.

Take for instance, our poor harried mother who has been our example before. Since she has discovered that the usual methods of trying to get her children to pick up their toys and belongings isn't working, it's time for her to attack the problem from a new angle. Perhaps instead of being both watchdog and nagger, she could appoint an older child, or appoint a different child each week, to be the toy inspector. She could furnish him a hat and badge and entrust him with the responsibility to make sure toys are put away. If he does a good job, he could earn an ice cream at the end of the week. Not only would this relieve the mother of some of the responsibility and hassles, but it would get the children involved in the problem and the solution.

In summary, solution-oriented problem solving is approaching a problem by identifying the problem, defining what you would like to see happening, and determining those steps that will take you there. Creative thinking and lateral thinking enhance one's ability to determine those steps.

An easy way to implement solution-oriented problem solving is to make a special section for it in the notebook used for planning your goals and objectives. Designate a section for problem solving and fill it with paper. Each night, or during your weekly planning session, or whenever you feel the need, turn to that section and write down the problem you are concerned about. Then write down what you would like to see happening. Next, take a few minutes to see if there are some logical steps that bridge the gap between what is now happening and what you want to see happening. If you cannot think of any steps, ask yourself some "what-if" questions and ponder the implications of your answers. Also, ask yourself if there is an easier, more creative approach to solving your problems. Is there a back door to your problem or an open window? Then write down the steps you've come up with.

To give you an example of how this works, here is an entry from one of the pages in my problem solving section:

A. Problems

  1. I feel like there is too much to do, I have too little time for myself.

  2. I'm too uptight about the house getting messed up.

  3. Lindsey's not doing her work.

B. Desired Results

  1. Have time for myself and not feel overwhelmed with things to do. Be relaxed enough to read to the kids and do impulsive, fun projects or outings.

2. Have a clean house *and* a happy spirit.

3. Have Lindsey do her work without complaining and without me getting upset.

C. Steps to Get from A to B

1. Don't commit all my time and energy to other people. Lower my expectations of the amount I can accomplish during the day. Put Clint down for naps and let him cry for ten minutes before going to him. (This was at a point where my seven-month-old baby wasn't taking any naps.)

2. Realize it's the kids' house too. Check on having someone help me clean. Clean a little each day instead of all in one day.

3. Remember Lindsey is two years younger than Steffany and that she needs more help. Help her whenever she asks, even when I think she should be able to do it by herself. Praise her more.

Being able to determine solutions to your problems creates a feeling of personal power. It eliminates the need for sympathy and replaces it with solutions. And it kindles an inner glow that comes from the knowledge that you can handle the problems and challenges of your life and in some cases eliminate them.

Effectiveness and Efficiency

In years past, the buzzword of American business was *efficiency.* There were efficiency experts, efficiency standards, and efficiency ratings. But soon, businessmen realized that efficiency, or the ability to get a lot of things done, was not enough. People needed to do more than get things done; they needed to get the *right* things done. So began the push for effectiveness.

As homemakers, it is important for us to learn from this

lesson from the business world. It is not enough to be busy all day long. We need to be doing the right things.

Effectiveness, or doing the right things, is largely a matter of setting priorities, and priorities are a natural result of planning backwards. By planning your year, month, week, and day, your priorities are constantly before you. It simply takes an extra minute when planning to determine which things are the most important things to do that day.

This can be done by simply starring those things that are most important or by assigning them an *A, B, C* (or 1, 2, 3) value. Items you designate as *A* are those things that need to be done that day or as soon as possible. *B* items are things that you would like to get done but are not pressing. *C* items are things that you'd like to do eventually.

Once you have assigned each item a priority, it is important to do the *A* items before moving on to the *B* and *C* items, even when the *B* and *C* items are easier or more fun.

A prioritizing system makes being effective fairly simple and easy. The element that makes being effective challenging is that the right things are constantly changing. There is no priority list etched in stone that says what things should always be done first, second, and third. These things change as different needs arise and when different deadlines come to the forefront.

So how do we deal with ever-fluctuating priorities? Firstly, we need to be flexible. We need to allow our *A, B,* and *C* items to shift in importance when the need arises. For instance, let's presume that mopping the kitchen floor had been a *B* item for a few days, but the glass of lemonade that was just spilled elevated it to an *A* level. If, however, your baby awakes while you are getting out your mop, and he is burning up with a fever, mopping the floor is suddenly thrust back down to a *B*, as may be many other *A* items.

Secondly, to deal with ever-fluctuating priorities, we need

to frequently review our life's purpose and our yearly, monthly, and daily goals. By doing so, we keep our priorities constantly in mind. Then when a responsibility with a deadline demands our time and energy, we can momentarily shift our emphasis to that responsibility with confidence that our shift in energy is only momentary and that we can shift back to those things that are the most important upon meeting our deadline.

Keeping our goals in mind will also help us recognize those times when we must say no to certain commitments so that we do not neglect that which is truly most important.

Thirdly, we need to balance our energy and time between the different *A* items. This is often difficult to do because we strive to fill so many roles and try to do each perfectly. So often, we spend hours working with and teaching our children, cleaning our houses, and preparing meals and Relief Society lessons. At the end of the day, we fall into bed exhausted and depressed that out of the past seventeen hours we were not able to somehow, somewhere, squeeze out some time for ourselves. Or sometimes we take time for personal interests and neglect our other responsibilities and end up fulfilled, but ridden with guilt.

The key is balance. We need to meet all our different needs, even if it means meeting them all at a sixty percent level instead of meeting one at one hundred percent, two at fifty percent, and one not at all. In order to clean the house, spend time with our children, and have time for ourselves, we may need to forego cleaning the baseboards or straightening the closet. By doing so, we can create a half hour to read a favorite novel, take a bubble bath, or do something just for ourselves.

Chances are that every single day will not be a perfectly balanced day. It doesn't need to be. There can be days where we spend most of our time on church work if there are also days where we spend much of our time with our children or doing something for ourselves. But on the whole, we need to strive for balance. Otherwise, our life will become warped. Just like the music of a warped record is distorted and unpleasant, the music of our lives will be distorted and unsatisfying.

As we strive for effectiveness in our daily lives, we must not confuse effectiveness with being busy. Remember, effectiveness is not doing "something" every minute of the day. Effectiveness is doing the right things. Many of the ways a mother is most effective are not measurable. For instance, after playing with your children or reading them books for an hour, there is no tangible evidence that your time has been gainfully employed. There is no cake that has been baked, no shining floor, and no dress that has been made. But there is invisible evidence of time well spent. There is the increased feeling of love and closeness. This feeling is infinitely more important than a cake, which lasts a few days.

Because of the many things that must be done to physically care for a family and to keep a home running smoothly, the ideal is a blend of efficiency and effectiveness. We need to be efficient when it comes to task-oriented activities such as laundry, cleaning, and meal preparation. And we need to be effective when it comes to relationship-oriented activities with our children and spouse. This blend of efficiency and effectiveness will enable us to take care of the physical needs of our family and their higher, intangible needs. It will also help us feel personal fulfillment from our very important careers as mothers.

Wise Investments

A wise businessman realizes that he needs to do more than work for money; he needs to make his money work for him. Therefore, he invests in stocks, bonds, real estate, and commercial ventures. He does not, however, do so haphazardly. He studies the market, the interest rates, the initial outlay of capital, and the proposed return. Upon this information, he makes his investment decision.

As mothers and homemakers, one of our most valuable commodities, often superseding money, is our time. The same principles that govern the wise investment of money pertain to the investment of our time. We need to assess the investment of our time, just as a wise money investor would do, according to the initial outlay and the likely return.

There are basically four categories of time investments. Three of the four kinds of time investments are valuable at different times for different kinds of projects. One of the kinds of time investments should be avoided completely. Let's take a closer look at these categories.

The first kind of time investments are minimum-minimum investments. These are the tasks and activities that require relatively little time. They can be completed quickly and easily. However, the return on the investment is proportionate to the time invested. For instance, a poster that can be made in ten minutes may not be the most dazzling or artistic, but it can get the message across. A quick run through at a car wash may not get the bumpers shiny, the white walls scrubbed, or the inside vacuumed, but it can get the bugs off the headlights and the cat's muddy footprints off the hood.

Because of the vast number of demands on our time, the minimum-minimum investment is necessary for some things. However, it should not be used for everything.

The second kind of time investments are maximum-minimum investments. These are the things that require a great deal of time but have a very small return. These are the most futile of all investments and should be eliminated. And yet, it seems that often in our church callings we get caught up in this kind of investment. We spend hours making a darling handout for Relief Society that everyone looks at and says, "How cute," then promptly forgets it, throws it away, or lets their baby mangle it. We spend an hour on a flyer when ten minutes would do. And we choose decorations that require hours of intricate handwork, when simpler decorations could be used.

These kind of maximum-minimum activities have been going on for years and are almost expected in certain church callings. And while I hate to do it, I must plead guilty of several maximum-minimum investments in my past years of church service. For instance, there was the time I was the ward newsletter editor and I spent four hours calling two-thirds of the children in Primary to find out why they loved their father for our June Father's Day issue. There was the time we hand delivered our first newsletter in 110 degree weather to each of the families in our ward to make sure they received it.

The most classic example of all, and I am still chagrined when I think of it, is the time I spent three days making gingerbread wagons with rosette wheels for centerpieces for a Relief Society dinner. I suffered both burned fingers and frustration trying to glue the gingerbread wagon pieces together with melted sugar, only to have them fall apart. I eventually had to glue them with Elmer's glue and put popcorn in the wagons just to cover up all the mistakes. They turned out presentable, but they did not justify all the hours of work or frustration.

Sometimes we feel that by doing all of these little things we are truly magnifying our calling. But there are many ways to magnify our callings without becoming involved in maximum-minimum activities. In fact, our effectiveness might increase if we use the time spent on maximum-minimum activities to sharpen our teaching skills, prepare our lesson, or make contact with our students.

It is not only in our church callings that we make

maximum-minimum investments. There are many times we do it as mothers and homemakers. There are dinners that no one likes yet take two hours to prepare, dresses that take several hours to sew but are never worn, and games that are made but are never played with.

Generally, we don't purposefully embark upon a maximum-minimum activity. We don't think, "This is going to take a lot of time, and it won't be worth it, but I'll do it anyway." Rather, we fail to completely think through a project and to accurately assess the time involved and the probable results. We start on a project full of good intentions and grand expectations and meet reality only when we have expended too much energy to back out.

Consequently, we can eliminate most maximum-minimum activities by carefully evaluating activities before we get involved in them on the basis of their results. Instead of thinking "Will this be cute?" we need to ask ourselves such questions as "How much time will this take? Will this be remembered more than momentarily? Is there something just as effective that can be done with less time or money?" These kinds of questions will help us eliminate maximum-minimum activities before we become involved in them.

The third kind of time investments are maximum-maximum investments. These are the activities that take a great deal of time and energy but the result is magnificent, effective, or worth the effort. These kinds of activities are essential for certain things, but we should become involved in them selectively. If we make every activity a maximum-maximum activity, we will soon be overwhelmed.

In some areas of our church callings we might want to make a maximum-maximum investment. For instance, once when I was in the Primary presidency, the stake Primary asked us to strive for a hundred percent attendance during the month of April. We felt impressed that for our ward we needed a little more than just a push for attendance, so we initiated a program we called "Reaching the One." We had a special presentation of our program during an in-service meeting. We asked each teacher to commit to choosing one child that had not come regularly or needed special attention and to make contact with that child once a week for the next month. We contacted the home teachers of each of these children to let them know of our efforts and to ask them to encourage the child to come to Primary during their home teaching visit. To show that as a presidency we were willing to do what we were asking the teachers to do, we promised to contact each of the teachers each week with a special reminder of our "Reaching the One" program and to also check on their progress with their student. This was in addition to the hundred percent attendance we were working on with the children.

The next month turned out to be a very busy one. Much time and energy was spent on making clever reminders and checking with the teachers. We definitely invested a maximum amount of time and energy. At the end of the month, we discovered our attendance had increased by ten percent, but more importantly, twelve of our twenty inactive children had come to Primary. Our investment of time and energy had been a maximum one, but so was the return on our investment.

There are certain maximum-maximum activities that we need to be involved in as mothers. One that I feel is essential in our home is teaching our children to work. It definitely consumes a great deal of time to teach a three-year-old how to properly scour a sink and then to work with and supervise that child until he can do it correctly. It takes a great deal of energy to teach a five-year-old how to sweep the kitchen floor and end up with more crumbs in the dustpan than on the floor. It takes a great deal of patience to listen to moans, groans, and complaints every day about these strenuous, demanding tasks. And it definitely takes a great deal of commitment to spend three hours doing work that you can do in forty-five minutes. But the return on this investment is also a maximum one. Eventually, complaints will ebb, efficiency will speed up, and one day somewhere in the future, our children will really be good helpers. They will also have learned self-discipline, industry, and responsibility.

When investing in maximum-maximum activities, there is a danger that it will turn into a maximum-minimum one. However, as long as we make a careful pre-activity assessment, we must simply accept it as an investment risk. Plus, there are times we do not see all of the returns on our investments. What started as a maximum-maximum activity and seemed to turn into a maximum-minimum one, may in the long run prove to truly be a maximum-maximum one.

Generally, the most ideal, profitable investment is a minimum-maximum investment. This is the kind that consumes a minimum amount of time and energy but still returns effective, desirable results. Examples of such investments are making a simple child's dress that is worn over and over, making a dinner that is easy to make and everyone enjoys, and even wearing your hair in a style that is attractive yet easy to fix.

We should try to utilize minimum-maximum investments as much as possible. If you are having several people over for dinner, consider your menu in terms of the minimum-maximum investment principle. For instance, the time investment of making eclairs for dessert, making ice cream sundaes, or even buying eclairs is all quite different. In terms of results, the homemade eclairs would probably be the most impressive, but would they warrant the hours required to make them? And if money is an element to be considered, which would be the cheapest and still delicious and appropriate?

There are many ways we can use the principle of minimum-maximum investments in our church callings. For instance, as a Primary presidency we found that to let our teachers know we appreciated their work, a simple postcard with a sticker and a brief message was a perfect minimum-maximum gesture. We could have done many other darling, more time-consuming things, and occasionally we did, but we found the postcards were effective yet easy to do. Because they required a minimum investment of time, it was something we could do frequently.

Another Primary activity that was a minimum-maximum activity was making edible covered wagons for a July 24th activity day. These edible wagons were a far cry from the fragile gingerbread wagons with delicate rosette wheels. These were made with Fig Newtons for the wagon, a large marshmallow for the cover, and little candies for the wheels. These were assembled with a dab of frosting, which we let the children do. Of all the ingredients, only the frosting had to be made and the chances of error in assembling them were slight. All we had to do was to supervise the children and then hand them their wagon on their way *out* of the building.

The minimum-maximum principle does not always mean that we choose the easiest, least time-consuming activity. Rather, we should choose the easiest activity that will give us the best results. For instance, for the Primary activity day, it would have been easier to simply hand the children a sugar cookie as they left, but we felt that letting the children make something offered a better return on our investment of time than just handing them something. Plus, we felt that the seasonal appropriateness of an edible covered wagon justified a little extra time.

In choosing an activity that requires a minimum amount of time for the maximum return, we are not being mediocre, unambitious, or stingy with our time. We are not forsaking the quality of our result merely for something that does not require much time or effort. Rather, we are choosing the least time-consuming activity that still gives us good results. And when we choose more time-consuming activities, we are making sure that the end result is worth the increased time spent.

The one element of time investment that we have not yet considered is the element of enjoyment. If there is something that we really enjoy doing, the enjoyment, though intangible, should be figured into the return. For instance, if a visiting teacher really enjoys doing counted cross-stitch, it might be a good investment of time for her to make a counted cross-stitch item as a Mother's Day gift for each of the women she visits. While a card or loaf of bread might have the same effect and take less time, the counted cross-stitch gives her a maximum return on her investment of time because it is something she enjoys doing.

To make investments that require a minimum amount of time and yield a maximum return, we should pre-evaluate activities according to probable results. The following questions could help you to do this:

1. How much time will this take?
2. How much time will this take if something goes wrong?
3. Will this be remembered more than momentarily?
4. Is there something just as effective that can be done with less time or money?
5. What would require the least investment of time and energy and still return a satisfactory result?
6. What simplifications can reduce my investment of time and energy?
7. Is the extra effort in proportion to the extra return?

Answering these questions before we become involved in a project or activity will help us use our time in the most effective way and help us turn many of our minimum-minimum, maximum-minimum, and maximum-maximum activities into minimum-maximum ones.

True Professionalism

My husband has often made the comment that there are relatively few true professionals in many jobs. We met one once in a furniture store. She was a woman who really listened to what we said, offered interior decorating advice, and followed up with several personal phone calls. We met another when we had some linoleum laid in our bathroom. Not only did he do an excellent job, but he did more than we had asked him to do. We have run across a few more true professionals. But frequently, we run into people who are just doing a job, who are more interested in finishing than excelling, who do what is necessary but no more. Many of these people do their job well, but that is all.

The true professional is the person who, because of his drive for personal excellence, does more than he is obligated to do and more than he is paid for. Recently I found a person who is such a professional. I first met him at church, or he met me. I had spent most of the meeting standing in the back of the chapel while I wrestled with a baby whose greatest desire was to crawl up to the podium. As soon as the meeting ended, a gentleman I had never seen before walked up to me and said, "Your hair looks really nice. I should know, I'm a hair designer." He smiled and walked away.

I had met many people who cut hair. There are many more who are haircutters. But this was the first person I met who was a hair designer. His professional attitude about his work impressed me, as did his special effort to offer a compliment that could have just as easily gone unsaid. I didn't even know him. I had to point him out to my husband the next Sunday just to learn his name. Because of his professional attitude and his extra effort, I remembered him and when I was ready for my next haircut, I went to him.

When I walked into the salon, he greeted me by name and shook my hand. He then washed my hair before having me sit down for the haircut. Then he did what I had never seen a beautician do before; he paused and stared at me. I was a little uncomfortable under his minute scrutiny, but I was more puzzled. My bewilderment apparently showed on my face for he raised his finger and said, "Just a minute. I'm studying the contours of your face." In a few moments, he suggested the kind of hairstyle he felt would look best on me and explained what elements of my facial structure supported his decision.

As he began cutting, he offered this explanation: "You see, I sculpt hair. I must study the way your hair lies and the contours of your face in order to give you your best possible cut. I want you to look your best when you walk out of here because you are an advertisement for me and my work, and I take great pride in my work."

As he cut and worked with my hair, his pride of craftsmanship became apparent. He took time to study my hair and was meticulous while he snipped and trimmed. Each cut reflected his pride and desire for personal excellence. By the end of my haircut, I realized I had met a true professional.

As mothers and homemakers, we need this professional attitude about our career. Without this professional attitude, this pride of craftsmanship, we raise kids and clean houses. With it, we sculpt souls and create environments of order that are conducive to love and learning.

It is through this professional attitude, by taking pride in our career and in the quality of our work and by being committed to personal excellence, that we will obtain personal fulfillment from the greatest, most far-reaching career we will ever have.

Herbert Hoover once said, "The great danger facing the American people is the possibility of our developing a cult of mediocre individuals." As full-time mothers and homemakers, we are engaged in a career in which it is crucial for us to rise above mediocrity and strive for excellence. Applying the principles of solution-oriented problem solving, effectiveness and efficiency, wise investment of our time, and commitment to personal excellence can help us do so. As we strive for excellence, we will find great satisfaction and fulfillment. Of this fulfillment, N. Eldon Tanner said, "I wish to say without equivocation that a woman will find greater satisfaction and joy and make a greater contribution to mankind by being a wise and worthy mother raising good children than she could make in any other vocation."[6] This is indeed a great promise for a great career.

ATTAINING HAPPINESS

*D*uring the early days of the American Republic, Benjamin Franklin spoke many times on the Constitution of the United States. After one stirring speech, an uncouth fellow rose and boldly walked a few paces toward the platform. "Aw, them words don't mean nothin' a-tall!" he shouted at Franklin. "Where's all the happiness you say it guarantees us?"

"My friend," replied Mr. Franklin, "the Constitution only guarantees the American people the right to pursue happiness. You have to catch it yourself."[1]

This anecdote from the life of Benjamin Franklin illustrates an important truth: Each of us holds the responsibility for our own happiness. But how seriously do we take this responsibility?

The statesmen who drafted the United States Constitution considered happiness so important they listed the pursuit of happiness as an inalienable right, like unto life and liberty. Robert Louis Stevenson said, "No duty is so underrated as the duty of being happy." And the Lord has stated that the purpose of our existence is to have joy.

In spite of the importance of happiness, many of us sacrifice our happiness as we become involved in other pursuits like cleaning our house, raising our children, and fulfilling our church responsibilities. This is truly ironical for the real purpose behind these activities is to create happiness. Consequently, we need to take a closer look at happiness and how to be happy.

The Nature of Happiness

Happiness has been defined as "a state of mind in which our thinking is pleasant a good share of the time."[2] Notice the definition does not say happiness is good health, money, a beautiful home, or a gorgeous figure. These are *things.* Happiness is a state of *mind.*

Of course, certain things can stimulate a person to have happy, pleasant thoughts. Take for instance a woman who buys a beautiful dress she has frequently admired and longed for. When she walks out of the store, she is not carrying a box of happiness. She is carrying a thing. It just so happens that because of this thing, she is choosing to think happy thoughts.

We need to understand that happiness does not come from things but from the thoughts we choose to think. If we fail to make this distinction, we build our happiness on a very wobbly foundation. And when we lose our things or when their newness wears off and we tire of them, the foundation of our happiness crumbles and we cease to be happy.

The *things* we are talking about upon which people frequently base their happiness are things like money, a beautiful home, a swimming pool, a microwave oven, or a new vacuum. The list goes on and on. Also on this list are things which are not necessarily tangible objects, such as a different church calling, more free time, or success. While these may not be accurately categorized as things, they are external concepts upon which people base happiness.

But none of these things, tangible or intangible, ensure happiness. There are many people who have had money, talent, and fame and yet commit suicide because they are unhappy. There are many other people, including kings and millionaires, who apparently have everything and yet live a life nearly devoid of happiness. The Caleph Abdelraham is attributed with saying: "I have now reigned above fifty years in victory or peace, beloved of my subjects, dreaded by my enemies, and respected by my allies. Riches and honors, power and pleasure, have waited on my call. Nor does any earthly blessing appear to have been wanting to my felicity. In this situation, I have diligently numbered the days of pure and genuine happiness which have fallen to my lot, and they amount to fourteen."[3]

Material things and worldly recognition do not ensure happiness, and conversely, the lack of material things does not preclude happiness. In the early days of the Church, the Saints suffered nearly every persecution imaginable. Husbands and fathers were falsely imprisoned, beaten, and tarred and feathered with tar to which acid had been added in order to burn their skin. Many were murdered. Families were terrorized and scattered in the middle of winter. They were driven from one place to another, and in the process their homes were burned, their land and properties confiscated, and their possessions destroyed. They were stripped of all of their material goods. Yet, John Taylor remarked, "I never saw a time that the Saints enjoyed themselves better than when they, apparently, were wading through their deepest troubles."[4]

The underlying premise of these examples is not that having things makes one unhappy and that not having things ensure happiness. Rather, happiness exists independently of external sources such as material goods, because happiness is a state of mind.

We Control Our Thoughts

"The power to think," says Bruce R. McConkie, "is an inheritance which all men receive because they are the spirit children of an Omnipotent Father."[5] In addition to this great gift, God has given us another gift to be used in conjunction with the power to think. This gift is free agency.

Free agency is the very principle upon which all of creation and salvation is based. It was decreed and in effect before the foundations of this earth were laid. We were endowed with free agency and given the opportunity to use it by choosing between Christ's plan of salvation or Satan's plan of compulsion.

In our mortal existence, we have the agency to choose between right and wrong and good and evil. We "are free to choose liberty and eternal life, through the great Mediator of all men, or to choose captivity and death, according to the captivity and power of the devil." (2 Nephi 2:27.) In addition to free agency of action, we also have the free agency of thought. We can choose what we will think and no one can take away that right unless we voluntarily relinquish it.

Prisoners of war learned that their enemies could exert power over their bodies. They could torture and torment them until they would give classified information. They could coerce and threaten them until they would sign affidavits they didn't believe in; but they could not control their thoughts.

Captain Larry Chesley, who was a prisoner in Hanoi, recounts that the North Vietnamese tried to force the prisoners to recognize "the truth," or their political beliefs. But, says Captain Chesley, "They apparently could not understand that we had minds of our own and that we really approved of and gloried in the right to dissent which was our birthright as Americans. Apparently too they could not or would not understand that a person cannot be forced to believe something, however much he may be constrained to give verbal agreement."[6]

We alone control our thoughts. And with this God-given

power of control, also comes the *responsibility* to control our thoughts.

From the scriptures we know we are to cast away idle thoughts (D&C 88:69), to forsake unrighteous thoughts (Acts 8:18–24), to think virtuous thoughts (D&C 121:45), and to think upon the things of God (Mosiah 5:13). Since we have also been informed that the purpose of our existence is to have joy, it follows that our responsibility to think happy thoughts is also divine.

To fulfill this divine responsibility, we must begin at the very foundation of happiness, which is inner peace and serenity.

The Happiness of Inner Peace

Happiness takes many forms. There is the happiness of anticipation that is visible in a child's eyes on December 20. There is the happiness of recreation, the happiness of achievement, and the happiness of friendship, to name just a few. The basic of all forms of happiness is the happiness of inner peace. Without this happiness, all other forms of happiness are but fleeting moments of pleasure. With it, the other forms of happiness have depth and significance. This happiness of inner peace comes from being true to God and self.

One of the fiercest rebukes Christ delivers in the New Testament is to the Pharisees. This scathing rebuke, recorded in Matthew 23, is delivered because the Pharisees were not true to God. At the time of Christ, the Pharisees were the spiritual leaders of the Jewish community. It was their duty to explain the Jewish doctrine and to administrate the religious law.[7] In doing so, they were exacting and meticulous. They required all to comply with every jot and tittle of the Mosaic law.

They themselves were flawless in upholding the ceremonious aspects of the Law of Moses. They performed the
intricate washings to wash away the impurities that perhaps
might defile their hands through contact with unclean platters
and cups. They paid tithes of mint, anise, and cummin. And
they engaged in lengthy prayer.

In spite of their dedication to the ceremonious aspects of
the law, their righteousness was hollow. They ignored the
weightier matters of justice, mercy, and faith. They endeavored
to appear to be true to God, but they were in reality deceitful
and covetous. Christ boldly denounced this hypocrisy when
he said: "Woe unto you, scribes and Pharisees, hypocrites! for
ye are like unto whited sepulchres, which indeed appear
beautiful outward, but are within full of dead men's bones,
and of all uncleanness. Even so ye also outwardly appear
righteous unto men, but within ye are full of hypocrisy and
iniquity." (Matthew 23:27–28.) A more repulsive simile could
not have been chosen. Whitewashed sepulchres were but
encasements for rotting flesh and dead men's bones.[8]

Six other times in the same discourse Christ denounces
the scribes and Pharisees as hypocrites and twice he calls
them fools and blind. They merited and received this harsh
reprobation because in spite of their pretense of devotion, in
their hearts they were not true to God.

Their unfaithfulness to God not only brought upon them
the stinging words of Christ, but it denied them peace, which
is reflected by the numerous and intricate plots and plans they
conceived in order to hopefully bewilder Christ or force him
to utter inconsistencies. They were troubled enough that they
even joined with the opposing factions, the Sadducees and
the Herodians, in these efforts. (See Matthew 22:15–29.) They
were concerned enough about Christ and his influence that
they stooped to perjury and blatantly illegal judicial proce-
dures and then took their case to the Roman government to

plead for execution. Their worry did not cease with Christ's death, as evidenced by their appeal to Pilate to put a watch at Christ's tomb. They lacked the peace and happiness that comes from being true to God.

In comparison, consider Joseph Smith. After he received the First Vision he was bitterly persecuted and reviled. Yet even as a youth, his commitment to stand true to God was unwavering. He writes: "I had actually seen a light and in the midst of that light I saw two Personages, and they did in reality speak to me; and though I was hated and persecuted for saying that I had seen a vision, yet it was true; and while they were persecuting me, reviling me, and speaking all manner of evil against me falsely for so saying, I was lead to say in my heart; Why persecute me for telling the truth? I have actually seen a vision; and who am I that I can withstand God, or why does the world think to make me deny what I have actually seen? For I had seen a vision; I knew it, and I knew that God knew it, and I could not deny it, neither dared I do it; at least I knew that by so doing I would offend God, and come under condemnation." (Joseph Smith—History 1:25.)

Joseph Smith remained true to God and consequently had an inner peace. He retained this peace in spite of persecution and even in the face of death. In Doctrine and Covenants 135:4, we read: "When Joseph went to Carthage to deliver himself up to the pretended requirements of the law, two or three days previous to his assassination, he said, 'I am going like a lamb to the slaughter; but I am calm as a summer's morning; I have a conscience void of offense towards God, and towards all men."

This same inner peace is available to us if we remain true to God by living the principles of the Gospel of Jesus Christ.

The next step in establishing the happiness of inner peace is being true to ourselves. To be true to ourselves, we need to be true to the ideals and standards we have personally chosen. History gives many examples of men who have so lived. Perhaps one of the greatest of all is Socrates. Socrates lived in Athens from about 470 to 399 B.C. He was the first of the great ancient Greek philosophers who laid the foundations of Western philosophy. In 399, Socrates was indicted for, among other things, the "corruption of the young." He answered this charge by saying, "For I do nothing but go about persuading you all, old and young alike, not to take thought for your persons and your properties, but first and chiefly to care about the greatest improvement of the soul."

So strongly did Socrates believe in these principles, upon which he based his own life, that he also said: "O men of Athens, I say to you, do as Anytus bids or not as Anytus bids, and either acquit me or not; but whatever you do, know that I shall never alter my ways, not even if I have to die many times."[9] And because of his stand, Socrates did have to die by drinking the fatal hemlock.

Proof of Socrates' inner peace and contentment is written in the Crito which details the scene shortly before Socrates' death. In this scene Crito says, "I have always thought you happy in the calmness of your temperament; but never did I see the like of the easy, cheerful way in which you bear this calamity."[10] As it was for Joseph Smith, Socrates' peace and tranquility transcended opposition and death.

Another example of being true to one's personal principles of integrity comes from the life of Gerhardt, a little German shepherd boy.

In a 1977 *Ensign* article entitled "Integrity," N. Eldon Tanner related a story about a little German shepherd boy named Gerhardt. It seemed that Gerhardt was very poor, and one day while he was tending his flock of sheep, a hunter came out of the woods and asked the way to the nearest village. Gerhardt explained how to get to the village, but the hunter wanted him to show him and said that he would pay

Gerhardt handsomely. Even after the hunter offered to pay him more than he had earned in a year, Gerhardt refused, saying that he had to stay and watch his sheep. It soon became known that the hunter was in fact the grand duke, and he was so pleased with Gerhardt's honesty that he later sent for him and had him educated. Although Gerhardt eventually became a powerful and wealthy man, he remained honest and true.[11]

Gerhardt was not called upon to sacrifice his life for his principles nor was he called upon to endure suffering or persecution. Rather, he was challenged to remain faithful to his personal standards while caring for his sheep. It is much the same for mothers and homemakers. The ways in which we will most often be called upon to be true to ourselves and our principles will probably be small ways, such as being honest with our children, sticking to the exercise program we have committed ourselves to, and keeping our houses in accordance to our personal standard of excellence. Or perhaps like Gerhardt, we may be challenged by the world to forsake our sheep for money or "fulfillment."

The little, daily ways in which we are true to ourselves may not move a mountain or change a world, but being true to ourselves even in small ways will create a feeling of peace and happiness, which is the foundation for all other forms of happiness.

Happiness Amidst Crises

While expecting our third child, I ran across the following quote, "When you are thinking happiness you are happy, regardless of what you are doing or what your reality is at the moment."[12] When I read this, I saw more than words on a page. It was as if the words shouted, "Pay attention to me. I am important!" Perhaps it had such a tremendous impact on me because I was anticipating labor and delivery or perhaps it was simply the fundamental truth of the statement.

I copied it in calligraphy and placed it in a prominent place in my bedroom so I could read it nightly. I used it as my focal point every time I practiced my breathing and relaxation exercises. I even put it in a frame and took it to the hospital when I went into labor. In fact, it was one of the first things I put in my suitcase.

This concept of thinking happiness regardless of what is going on around us applies to more than delivering a baby. It applies to all facets of life, no matter how disagreeable or difficult the circumstances are. As mothers and homemakers, we get our share of disagreeable and difficult circumstances. There are hundreds of dirty diapers, and children who hold you tight and say, "Mommy, I feel like I'm going to throw up," just before they do—all over you. Beyond the less desirable parts of mothering, there are the crises, things like pneumonia, broken arms, and the threat of miscarriage that sends you to bed for two months. These are not only physically draining, but emotionally draining as well.

But even in difficult circumstances, we still have control over our thoughts. As Shakespeare wrote in Hamlet, "For there is nothing good or bad but thinking makes it so." Thus, we can remain happy regardless of the situation if we choose to think happy thoughts.

Thinking happy thoughts is not always easy when things aren't going the way we want them to. Sometimes it's hard to even want to be happy. It's a lot easier just to get mad or frustrated. At these times, laughing is one of the best ways to get back to the point where we are capable and desirous of choosing happy thoughts.

Dr. Herman Ryber, a psychologist, pointed out at a physician's seminar that "laughter and the awareness of humor become doubly important when individuals are in abnormal, nonhumorous, situations. Unit commanders during World War II, for instance, felt that the situation was under control—despite mud, weariness, death, and danger—when the G.I.s under their command could still find something to laugh about."[13]

No mother would debate that there are times she must deal with mud, weariness, and danger (who wouldn't agree that having a birthday slumber party for ten twelve-year-olds isn't dangerous?), and that there are some very nonhumorous situations. But being able to laugh at these times can help us get the situation under control.

I discovered this one afternoon while I was washing clothes. I opened the washer and pulled out my husband's favorite pair of cream-colored corduroy pants. To my horror, they were no longer cream-colored, but pink. Determined to restore the corduroys to their original color, I ran them through another wash, and another, and another. After the third wash they were still pink.

My first impulse was to cry. But I restrained that impulse and followed my second impulse: to call my mother. On her advice, I proceeded to soak the pants in a solution of bleach and water. This was a tough stain; after all, it had resisted three washings. So if a half cup of bleach to a gallon of water was sufficient, surely one or even one-and-a-half cups of bleach would be better.

A few hours later, I pulled the pants up out of the water, and sure enough, I could see no trace of pink. What I did see was rust spots surrounding the metal button on the waistband. Upon closer examination, I discovered the rust spots were contagious; they had spread to all the material that had come in contact with the button.

Again in desperation I called my mom. This time she suggested lemon juice and sunlight. Looking in the refrigerator and out the window at the cloudy day, I realized that neither the lemons nor the sunshine were available, at least not before my husband came home from work and asked for his favorite pair of pants. Removing the stains by force seemed the best alternative. I scrubbed the rust stains with all the anger and frustration that churned inside me for having spent so much time and energy on one lousy pair of pants. Apparently my anger was substantial, for I removed the rust spots. I also removed the material. I stood in my kitchen and looked at my husband's favorite cream-colored pants, rusted and holey. And I laughed. The situation came under control and I knew what to do. I loaded up the kids and we went down to the store and bought my husband a new pair of favorite corduroy pants and put them neatly in his drawer.

Sometimes, situations are such that the only thing we can find to laugh about is the fact that one day we will laugh about it. One Saturday evening my husband and I got dressed up, though we wanted to stay in our work clothes and finish the projects we had been working on. We got a babysitter for the older kids, got our two-month-old baby dressed to go with us, packed into his diaper bag the numerous things that must go along with a two-month-old baby, and drove forty miles to a wedding. We had difficulty finding the home where the wedding was to be held. When we finally found it, we were perplexed by the lack of cars parked outside. While I put our baby's sweater on, my husband went up to the home to make sure it was the right place. In just a minute he yelled, "Amy, what was the date on the invitation?"

I responded, "It was today, September 30."

He walked back to the car and said, "Today is October 1."

The only response I had was, "Someday we'll laugh about this."

And we do.

When we can't quite laugh at a situation and we are unable to think happy thoughts, we can apply the principle President Kimball discusses in his book, *Faith Precedes the*

Miracle. He encourages us to build "reservoirs of faith so that when the world presses in upon us, we stand firm and strong; when the temptations of a decaying world about us draw on our energies, sap our spiritual vitality, and seek to pull us down, we [can draw on] a storage of faith that can carry youth and later adults over the dull, the difficult, the terrifying moments, disappointments, disillusionments, and years of adversity, want, confusion, and frustration."[14]

The same principle applies to building reservoirs of happiness. When we can't quite laugh at a situation and are unable to think happy thoughts, drawing on memories of happy times can help us cope.

Building reservoirs of happiness, learning to laugh, and realizing that we control our thoughts in every circumstance will help us be happy, even in the midst of crises.

The Happiness of Laughter

In the classic children's movie *Mary Poppins,* there is a scene where Mary Poppins and her wards visit Uncle Albert. They must rescue him from floating around the ceiling of his rather lofty parlor where he is suspended because of his uncontrollable laughter. When they arrive at Uncle Albert's home, they find the laughter is contagious, and they all float to the top of the parlor while laughing and giggling uproariously.

This fictional scene symbolizes what actually happens to our body when we engage in laughter, for "laughter is good for both body and mind. It eliminates nervous tensions which upset body functions and it clears the mind of annoyances and resentments. . . . Laughter leaves a feeling of well-being, of personal satisfaction, and of contentment."[15]

Laughter is a coping mechanism. It helps us deal with the physical and mental stress we encounter on a daily basis. We feel physically and mentally better for having laughed. Warren

Hinckle expressed the importance of laughter as a coping mechanism when he said, "Running around the outside of an insane society, the healthiest thing you can do is to laugh."

Mark Twain must have realized the importance of this, for he frequently created his own humor to laugh at. One day while at the races in England, he met a friend who complained he was broke and asked Mark Twain to buy him a ticket back to London.

"Well," Mark Twain said, "I'm nearly broke myself, but I'll tell you what I'll do. I'll buy one ticket and you can hide under my seat and I'll hide you with my legs." His friend agreed to this.

Then Mark went down to the ticket office and bought two tickets. When the train pulled out, his friend was safely under the seat. The conductor came around for the tickets and Mark gave him two. "For whom is this other ticket?" asked the bewildered conductor.

Tapping his head, the humorist said in a loud voice, "That is my friend's ticket! He is a bit eccentric and enjoys riding under the seat."[16]

We, too, can create our own humor to laugh at, or we can indulge in the comedy others provide. This sort of comedy abounds. There are comics in the newspaper, comedians on television and stage, and movies, books, and television shows that are humorous. Much of this kind of humor pokes fun at the foibles of society and everyday life. It is valuable in that it helps us to not take our own world so seriously.

Take for instance, the following excerpt from one of Erma Bombeck's books. After reading it, it is much easier to go back to mutiny at the dinner table and laugh. She writes: "My children always had an unusual diet. They tolerated hot dogs only when they cost $1.50 in the ballpark, hamburgers that were $1/15$-inch thick and suffocated in secret sauce, charred marshmallows that were speared on a bent coat hanger, and anything left under a car seat longer than fifteen days. . . . In general, they refused to eat anything that hadn't danced on TV."[17]

In addition to laughing at our world, we need to also learn to laugh at ourselves. Ethel Barrymore was a master at doing just that. One evening, she was in her dressing room in Hollywood when a studio usher tapped on the door. "A couple of gals in the reception room, Miss Barrymore, say they went to school with you. What shall I do?" he asked.

"Wheel them in," said the incomparable Ethel.[18]

Being able to laugh at ourselves and the world helps us cope with our world and its tensions and demands. It also opens the door to a very enjoyable and relaxing kind of happiness, the happiness of laughter.

The Happiness Habit

When we have discovered the happiness of inner peace, happiness amidst crises, and the happiness of laughter, the next step is to make happiness habitual. It has been estimated that ninety-five percent of our behavior, feeling, and response is habitual.[19] This indicates that if we are not thinking happy, pleasant thoughts much of the time, it is because we are not in the habit of doing so.

A lesson on the nature of habits can be learned from the book *Gulliver's Travels*. Gulliver is a doctor on board a ship that sails into a violent storm. Washed overboard, Gulliver resolutely swims—aided by fortune, wind, and tide—until he reaches a shore. He then falls on the beach exhausted and sleeps a deep and peaceful sleep. When he awakens, he finds he cannot move. He is bound from his armpits to his thighs with numerous strings. These bindings are just slender strings, one of which he could have easily broken. But there is not just one; there are many. And so he becomes the prisoner of a people who were only six inches tall.

It is much the same with habits. An act done once or twice is easy to break. But an act that is entrenched in our behavior pattern binds us. We become the prisoner of habit.

Because of the tremendous power of habits, Mark Twain says that habits are "not to be flung out of the window by any man, but coaxed downstairs a step at a time."[20] The easiest way to coax habits out of our life is to replace them with new habits.

One new habit that will help us establish the happiness habit is smiling. Once a little girl asked her mother if she was upset. Her mother replied, "No, dear, I'm not upset."

The daughter responded, "Then why haven't you told your face?"[21]

Many of us without even being aware of it pass the day, like this mother, with a lukewarm look. We neither bend our mouth up to a smile or down to a frown. We just let it be. And yet, the simple act of smiling can prompt happy feelings and thoughts. It's influence is almost immediate.

Smiling and its relationship to happiness is much like the controversy of "Which came first, the chicken or the egg?" We can just as well ask, "Which comes first, the smile or the happiness." Only this question can be answered and the answer is simple: both. At times, happiness stimulates the smile. At other times, the smile stimulates the happiness. The same is true for singing and whistling. Frequent smiling, singing, or whistling can help us establish the happiness habit.

Another activity that will help us establish the happiness habit is learning to enjoy simple pleasures. One day my mother called and told my daughter she found the button that had fallen off of her sweater. My daughter literally danced for joy. Then she ran and told her sister and then her father that grandma had found her button. I was amused by her joy over such a little thing and began to ponder the last time something as simple as a button prompted happiness for me.

As adults, we typically have forgotten to take pleasure in the little things. Our happiness has become more complex and sophisticated. This sophistication helps us strive for deeper, more lasting joys. But in our sophistication, we often cast aside the simple joys. We forget to feel the joy of a sunset, having our own home, and just being with our spouse, all of which at one time in our life were enough in and of themselves to stimulate very happy thoughts.

Returning to these simple pleasures requires us to slow down our hectic pace of life, at least momentarily, and take time to become aware again of the simple joys of life.

One last suggestion on how to establish the happiness habit is to begin now. When my daughter had just turned three, she frequently asked me, "Mom, is it tomorrow yet?" In her little mind, yesterday and tomorrow were as complicated to grasp as calculus. All that was real to her was today. It is unfortunate that many of us become so wise and knowledge-able in understanding the nature of time that yesterday and tomorrow become more real to us than today. Perhaps we would be better off if, in regards to happiness, we return to the childlike "confusion" of our past. After all, what we consider "confusion" may really be a superior understanding.

Joseph Smith said that "happiness is the object and design of our existence, and will be the end thereof, if we pursue the path that leads to it."[22] This pursuit is our opportunity and our responsibility. Among the paths that lead to it are being true to God and to self, which creates the happiness of inner peace, happiness amidst crises, the happiness of laughter, and the habit of happiness. By following these paths we will not only pursue happiness, but as Benjamin Franklin challenged, we will catch it.

DEVELOPING SPIRITUAL STRENGTH

Out of curiosity, I recently tried an experiment. I wrote down the top twelve things I spent my time and energy on. This list included such things as cleaning the house, teaching the children, being a companion to my husband, exercising and maintaining my physical appearance, and cooking the meals. I then gave the list to my husband and asked him to prioritize the items according to their importance to him. The comparison of his list to mine was very enlightening.

Later I thought how interesting it would be to see how Heavenly Father would prioritize such a list. How much variance would there be between his estimation of what's really important and mine. Would the things he considered most important even be on my list?

These musings brought me face-to-face with the questions, "How much time do I spend on increasing spirituality?" and "Just how important is it?" I found the answer to the second question in an *Ensign* article written by Joe J. Christensen. In it he stated: "With spirituality, we are successful, and without it we are not. It is that simple! Spirituality is the *sine qua non* (the without which [there is] not). . . . It is the key to true happiness and success in our lives in all kinds of circumstances."[1]

Surely, developing spirituality needs to be high on our list. Spirituality will help us resist the temptations of Satan. It will put us in touch with the Holy Ghost for personal revelation. And it will increase our level of faith. But the benefits of spirituality are not confined to spiritual areas; they spill over to every other aspect of our lives. With spirituality, we have greater wisdom in disciplining our children. We have a greater love within our marriage and have a greater ability for unselfishness and service for our husbands. We find greater joy and fulfillment in all we do. And spirituality creates inner strength.

Once we understand this, we must ask ourselves another question: "What is the best way to develop spirituality?" Undeniably we should look to Jesus Christ and follow his example.

The Strength of Prayer

Christ set the example of how to pray when he gave us the Lord's Prayer. He taught us to whom we pray, the attitude with which we approach the Father, and the kinds of things we should ask for. But with his life, he set other examples regarding prayer, including where to pray and how often.

Christ prayed frequently, often seeking the solitude of a mountain or an isolated place to commune with his Father. Mark records this about Jesus: "In the morning, rising up a great while before day, he went out, and departed into a solitary place, and there prayed." (Mark 1:35.) Matthew tells us of another occasion when Christ prayed: "When he had sent the multitudes away, he went up into a mountain apart to pray: and when the evening was come, he was there alone." (Matthew 14:23.) In solitary places, apart from worldly distractions and wondering men, Christ could share the contents of his soul and heart with his Father and draw from God's infinite wisdom and strength.

Christ prayed before partaking of food. He prayed for Peter that his faith would not fail. He prayed for his apostles that they would be kept from the evil of the world. Christ also prayed in preparation for spiritual events. Before he began his ministry, Christ spent forty days in the wilderness fasting and praying. Before he called his twelve apostles "he went out into a mountain to pray, and continued all night in prayer to God." (Luke 6:12.) And before he went to the Garden of Gethsemane, Christ prayed with and for his apostles.

Because Christ was no stranger to prayer, it was only natural that when he faced the most difficult episode of his mortal existence, he turned to prayer. During this episode, in the Garden of Gethsemane, when his suffering became so intense that great drops of blood dripped from his pores, he prayed more earnestly.

As mothers, we can learn much from the examples Christ set. We too can retreat to private closets, quiet bedrooms, or even locked bathrooms and share the contents of our hearts with our Eternal Father. We can pray for our children, our husbands, and our homes. We can pray for patience, wisdom, and ability. We can share our joys and our successes and express our sorrows, fears, and failures. And if we are not a stranger to prayer, when we encounter difficult times, it will be only natural for us to turn to prayer and there receive strength.

But prayer is not just a source of strength in times of crises. As Truman G. Madsen has said, prayer, at all times, "is mind-strengthening as well as soul-strengthening. It helps reorder our priorities and bring out into the open what otherwise only stirs and stagnates within."[2] But prayer can only do this if it's real prayer—the kind that is thoughtful and sincere, the kind that is free from interruptions as we wonder if we turned the water off or started the dishwasher. Prayers that are filled with mental wanderings or sleepy noddings have no power to strengthen or redeem. They are simply words muttered in a room. It is as Shakespeare wrote: "My words fly up, my thoughts remain below. Words without thoughts never to heaven go."[3]

These truths about prayer are well-known by most Latter-day Saints. The thing that is not so well-known is how to consistently have meaningful prayers. Too often we only have heartfelt prayers sporadically, usually when we need something. The other times, we intend to have meaningful prayers, but our thoughts get sidetracked or we are too tired to do more than mention the same old topics in the same old way.

Having personally struggled with the goal of consistently having meaningful prayers, I have tried different ways to improve my prayers. The thing I found the most helpful was applying a statement made by Lee Iacocca concerning goals. He said, "In conversation, you can get away with all kinds of vagueness and nonsense, often without even realizing it. But there's something about putting your thoughts on paper that forces you to get down to specifics."[4]

Applying this to my prayers, I began to write down specifically before I began to pray what I wanted to include in my prayers. While I was doing this, I could also clear my mind of distracting worldly concerns so I might focus on my prayer once I had started. I also found I began to consider my blessings in a more specific and thankful way.

As I did this, I found the vague and meaningless statements disappearing from my prayers. My prayers took on a new depth. When I finished each prayer, it was also easy to look back and ponder each thing I had prayed about. I was amazed to find how much inspiration I received each night if I simply took the time to really listen. This inspiration I also wrote down and later saved in a section in my planning notebook under the heading of "Inspiration to Govern my Life."

As long as I take the time to do this, prayer is a privilege. It is an opportunity to communicate with my Eternal Father and draw from his wisdom. It is a source of strength in my life. If I get too tired or busy to prepare for my prayer or to ponder what I prayed about, inevitably my prayers seem to lack efficacy.

We must do all we can to make sure our prayers are earnest, thoughtful communication and not just words bouncing off the ceiling, for only then is prayer a source of inner strength.

The Strength of Scriptural Knowledge

Another of Christ's sources of spiritual strength was his knowledge of the holy scriptures. With this knowledge, Christ rebuked his enemies, silenced their criticism, and escaped their verbal snares. Such was the case when the Pharisees denounced Christ for allowing his hungry disciples to pluck corn from the cornfields on the Sabbath day. Christ asked them if they had not read in the scriptures the account of David, who fleeing from an angered Saul ate the hallowed shewbread, which was set aside exclusively for the priests. Again referring to the scriptures, Christ said, "But if ye had known what this meaneth, I will have mercy, and not sacrifice, ye would not have condemned the guiltless." (Matthew 12:7.) The silenced Pharisees could not refute Christ's wisdom or knowledge of the scriptures.

Christ's knowledge of the scriptures gave him power not only to confound his mortal enemies, but to rebuff his greatest enemy of all—Satan. After Christ's baptism, but before he began his ministry, he was prompted by the Spirit to seek the seclusion of a wilderness where he could be free to commune with God. For forty days Christ remained in the wilderness, fasting and praying. Matthew tells us that Christ "communed with God, he was afterwards an hungered, and was left to be tempted of the devil." (JST, Matthew 4:2.) And

94

HOW TO FEEL GREAT ABOUT BEING A MOTHER

tempt him, Satan did. Ruthlessly choosing a moment of great physical weakness, Satan came to Christ with the insidious suggestion of using his godly powers to satisfy his physical appetite. Physically weak but spiritually strong, Christ responded by quoting scriptures. "It is written," he said, "Man shall not live by bread alone, but by every word that proceedeth out of the mouth of God." (Matthew 4:4.)

Undaunted, Satan returned to Christ, this time at the pinnacle of the temple. There he tempted Christ, "If thou be the Son of God, cast thyself down." The cunning adversary had not been repulsed by Christ without learning something. So this time when he tempted Christ, he himself used the scriptures. To his temptation, Satan added, "For it is written, He shall give his angels charge concerning thee: and in their hands they shall bear thee up, lest at any time thou dash thy foot against a stone." Ignoring the deliberate distortion of the scriptures, Christ answered Satan by again quoting scriptures: "It is written again, Thou shalt not tempt the Lord thy God." (Matthew 4:6–7.)

Again Satan came to Christ. This time Satan offered Christ the kingdoms of the world and all the power and glory of them. This temptation is supremely ironic. Here is Satan, who does not even have an earthly tabernacle, promising to give Christ the kingdoms and riches of the world. Christ created those kingdoms and riches. They were his and had he chosen to do so, he could have gathered them for himself. But Christ understood the nature of his messiahship. He realized that it did not include worldly power or temporal wealth. And so he rebuffed the tempter by again quoting the scriptures: "Thou shalt worship the Lord thy God, and him only shalt thou serve." (Matthew 4:10.)

Three times Satan tempted Christ in the wilderness and three times Christ answered his temptations by quoting scriptures. Christ knew the scriptures. He knew they testified of him. He knew the laws and commandments that he came to fulfill. But not only did he know the scriptures, he used them and drew strength from them to withstand the masterful temptations of Satan.

In a like manner, the scriptures can be a source of power and strength for us if we apply them in our life. They can help us in very specific ways in every facet of our lives. They can help us in our marriage, for as Spencer J. Condie said, "Any scripture counseling us on how to treat our fellowman is, by definition, inspired counsel on how married couples should treat each other."[5] With this in mind, the Sermon on the Mount takes on added meaning.

For instance, how often do we overlook our own flaws, but see our husband's with a magnifying glass? Yet Christ reminds us, "And why beholdest thou the mote that is in thy brother's [husband's] eye, but considerest not the beam that is in thine own eye?" Also in the Sermon on the Mount we are told, "Whosoever is angry with his brother [or husband] without a cause shall be in danger of the judgment." And how often should we forgive an offending spouse? Even seventy times seven, or in other words, there is no limit. (See Matthew 18:22.)

Consider also how applicable this counsel given to Oliver Cowdery is for both husbands and wives: "Therefore be diligent; stand by my servant Joseph, [or your spouse], faithfully, in whatsoever difficult circumstances he may be for the word's sake. Admonish him in his faults, and also receive admonition of him. Be patient; be sober; be temperate; have patience, faith, hope and charity." (D&C 6:18, 19.)

Any scripture proscribing conduct toward our fellowman could also apply to how we treat our children. Surely we need to be forgiving and slow to anger with our children as well as our husbands. There are other scriptures that can be applied to parenting. From Proverbs we learn that a soft answer turns away wrath, or temper tantrums. Also in Proverbs we learn we should "withhold not good from them to whom it is due." (Proverbs 3:27.) How easy it is to reprimand our children when they leave their rooms messy or when they fail to make their beds. But what about when they do these things? We must not withhold the praise that is due.

We can find further scriptural counsel on parenting by looking at the life of Christ. When his apostles returned from their missions, Christ took them aside to a solitary place. But the people knew where he went, and they followed him. Though probably anxious to discuss with his apostles their special missionary experiences and to further teach and bless them, Christ received the people. How do we respond when interrupted while trying to do something we really want to do? Do we receive our children lovingly, as Christ did?

Christ also set the example of how to handle children who have misbehaved and need to be punished. In the book of John we learn that early in his ministry, Christ went to Jerusalem for the Feast of the Passover. At the temple, he found greedy men turning sacred rites into base commerce. Their greed carried them and their animals right into the outer courts of the temple where they shouted the merits of the beasts, making the outer courts of the temple sound and look like a bazaar. Amidst the bleating of the sheep, the lowing of the oxen, and the shouting of the sellers was the clinking of money on scales that were not always just. So loud were all these noises that they disturbed the chant of the Levites and the prayers of the priests in the inner courts.[6]

Such was the condition of the holy temple of God, and it was a condition Christ would not tolerate. Filled with righteous indignation, Christ set about to clear the defiled temple. First he made a whip of small cords, an act that does not reflect impassioned, uncontrollable anger, and then he drove the sellers and their animals out of the temple. He drove out the moneychangers, poured out their money, and overturned their tables. Christ boldly denounced the corruption. He took immediate action, and he punished those who were responsible, but he never lost his self-control.

Within the scriptures there is also much advice on how we should manage our homes. We should be wise and thoughtful like the man who built a tower and beforehand counted the cost to make sure he would have sufficient to finish it. We should not be wasteful, but we should heed the example Christ set after feeding the five thousand. He commanded his disciples to "gather up the fragments that remain, that nothing be lost." (John 6:12.) And we should be like the five wise virgins and make sure our homes are well-supplied with the necessities of food, water, and clothing.

On a personal side, the scriptures tell us that we need to be organized and industrious. (See D&C 88:119–124.) We should "study and learn, and become acquainted with all good books, and with languages, tongues, and people." (D&C 90:15.) We are admonished to strive for self-mastery, for "he that hath no rule over his own spirit is like a city that is broken down, and without wall," and thus without defense from the enemy. (Proverbs 25:28.) And with all the things we are commanded to do, we are reminded that we don't have to do it all today, for "it is not requisite that a man should run faster than he has strength." (Mosiah 4:27.)

In every facet of our lives, the scriptures can give us insight and direction. But we cannot apply something we do not know. So our first step is to study the scriptures on a daily basis. We might choose to study a certain amount of pages or chapters a day or for a certain amount of time. We could read along with the Sunday School reading assignment. We could work through an institute manual or take an institute class. Whatever method we use is immaterial. What matters is that we do it.

In counseling the members of the Church to study the scriptures, Marion G. Romney said, "Don't let yourselves be too busy or too tired to [study]. The added strength, wisdom, and inspiration which comes therefrom will repay your efforts a thousand fold."[7] So often, being too busy or tired are the very things that hamper our efforts to daily scripture study. But if scripture reading gets crowded out by grocery shopping, running errands, taking a nap, or even church callings, we simply haven't made scripture reading a high enough priority.

When we give scripture study enough importance that we read daily, we will be blessed with strength, wisdom, and inspiration. We will find valuable ways to apply the scriptures in our daily lives. We will gain knowledge. And with that knowledge, we will also gain a feeling, a closeness to our Father, an awareness of spiritual things. In other words, as we study the scriptures we will gain spiritual strength.

Receiving a Fullness by Obedience

Another fundamental of spiritual strength is obedience. Again, it is Christ that set the supreme example. In Hebrews 5:8-9, Paul writes of Christ: "Though he were a Son, yet learned he obedience by the things which he suffered; and being made perfect, he became the author of eternal salvation unto them that obey him." Christ, himself, was subject to laws of heaven. And though he was the Son of God, he had to be obedient.

Obedience is the most basic of all spiritual principles. It is the condition for all blessings. It is the means by which we prove our love for Christ. It is, as Bruce R. McConkie says, "the first law of heaven, the cornerstone upon which all righteousness and progression rest."[8] It is also the prerequisite for spiritual power, for we must first prove our obedience before we qualify for greater spiritual strength.

For instance, a man must first be obedient to the

covenants he made at baptism before he can be privileged with the additional strength of the priesthood. We must be obedient to our previous spiritual covenants before we can enter into the greater covenants of the temple and enjoy the greater spiritual strength. Obedience both qualifies and prepares us for spiritual strength.

As we obey God's laws, many other things also happen. We receive blessings from God. We effect happiness. We prove our personal worthiness to enter into the presence of God. As Joseph F. Smith has said, "We keep in touch with God, and remain in harmony with his purposes."[9] And through our obedience, or lack of obedience, we reveal much about our commitment and our attitude.

For instance, much is revealed about Jonah's commitment by his response to the word of the Lord, which commanded him to "arise, go to Nineveh, that great city, and cry against it." (Jonah 1:2.) Jonah not only did not obey the Lord, but he found a ship that was going to Tarsus, a city that was over five hundred miles away from Nineveh. Eventually, he did hearken unto the word of the Lord, but his obedience came "by reason of [his] affliction" (Jonah 2:2), or the fact that he was within the belly of a great fish.

Much is revealed about the attitude of Naaman, the Syrian, by the wrath he felt at being commanded to do such a simple thing as wash in the river Jordan seven times to cure his leprosy. His subsequent humility, obedience, and gratitude also provides a deep insight into his character.

Much is revealed about the attitude of Laman and Lemuel by their response to the Lord's commandment to go back to Jerusalem to obtain the brass plates from Laban. They obeyed this commandment, but not without a great deal of murmuring and complaining about the difficulty of this task. Moreover, their behavior during this mission proved that in spite of outward obedience, within their hearts they were uncommitted, resentful, and rebellious. After successfully obtaining the plates from Laban and returning to Lehi, they were again commanded to return to Jerusalem. This time the purpose of their journey was to bring Ishmael's family to the wilderness so Lehi's sons might have wives. There was no murmuring, complaining, or hesitation to obey this commandment.

Much is revealed about the commitment of Nephi, who when commanded to build a ship did not question how or why or whether he could succeed at such a mammoth task. Instead he asked the Lord, "Whither shall I go that I may find ore to molten, that I may make tools to construct the ship?" (1 Nephi 17:9.)

Just as the behavior of Jonah, Naaman, Laman, Lemuel, and Nephi reveals much about their commitment to God and their spiritual attitude, our obedience to the commandments of God also reflects our commitment and attitude. Do we, like Jonah, ignore the word of the Lord when it is difficult or inconvenient to obey it? Do we, like Jonah, become humble and obedient only when compelled to do so by hardship or tragedy? Do we, like Naaman, belittle the importance of obeying commandments that are seemingly insignificant? Do we, like Laman and Lemuel, obey with half-hearted obedience? Do we, like Laman and Lemuel obey outwardly but harbor resentment inwardly? Or do we, like Nephi, obey without questioning how or why or our ability? Do we, like Nephi, pledge to "go and do the things which the Lord hath commanded" (1 Nephi 3:7) regardless of the difficulty of the commandment? Our answers to these questions reveal much about our spiritual attitude and our commitment to the Lord.

Obedience is an important way in which we can prove our spiritual attitude and commitment to the Lord. But since the Lord already knows the thoughts and intents of our hearts, perhaps the person who receives the greatest revelation is ourself. In his book *The Highest in Us,* Truman Madsen relates a conversation he had with Hugh B. Brown while they were in Israel. Together they stood in a valley where tradition has placed the tomb of Abraham. In this valley of great beauty and spiritual significance, Truman Madsen asked Hugh B. Brown: " 'What are the blessing of Abraham, Isaac, and Jacob?' Elder Brown thought a moment and answered in one word, 'Posterity.'

" 'Why, then was Abraham commanded to go to Mount Moriah and offer his only hope of posterity?' It was clear that this man, nearly ninety, had thought and prayed and wept over that question before. He finally said, 'Abraham needed to learn something about Abraham.' "[10]

What did Abraham learn? He learned that he loved God unconditionally. He learned he was truly committed to God. He learned that in spirit, mind, and heart he was submissive to the will of God. And perhaps he learned that he had a greater capacity for obedience than he ever before imagined.

So it is for us. As we prove our obedience to the Lord, we too learn much about ourselves. We learn about the level and degree of our commitment to God. We learn about our faith. We learn about our capacity for obedience. But not only do we learn about our capacity to obey, to commit, and to believe, we also strengthen that capacity. Thus as we obey, our ability to obey becomes greater. The greater our ability to obey, the greater our obedience. As this spiral continues, we increase our spiritual strength.

The Strength of Knowing Who We Are

Another source of Christ's spiritual strength was his knowledge of who he was and what he was to do. Before the foundations of this earth were laid, Christ was chosen to be the Savior of mankind. As the Savior, he would provide a way for all men to receive immortality and eternal life. This was a unique mission. No other person would be required to do this. To perform this unique mission, he would need a unique parentage. From one parent, he would need to inherit mortality so that he could be subject to temptation. He would have to be capable of sinning yet remain sinless in order to make the atoning sacrifice. From his mortal parent he would also need to inherit the ability to die so that he could give up his life. From the other parent, he would need to inherit immortality, giving him the "power to withstand death indefinitely"[11] so that his death would be voluntary, and giving him the power to reunite his body and spirit in a resurrected state.[12] And so, nearly two thousand years ago, Christ was born to a mortal mother and an immortal Father.

Like all others born into this world, a veil was drawn over Christ's mind at birth, obscuring the knowledge of premortal glories, his divine sonship, and his noble mission. Knowledge of these things came to him gradually.

By the time he was twelve, Christ knew he was the Son of God. This is evident by his experience in the temple. Christ had gone with Mary and Joseph to Jerusalem for the Feast of the Passover. When the feast ended, Mary and Joseph returned to Nazareth with their company or caravan. After traveling a day's journey, they discovered Jesus was not with them, nor was he with their family or friends. How easy it is to imagine the fear and concern in Mary's heart as they turned back to Jerusalem to search for her son. We can also imagine how this fear augmented as they searched fruitlessly for him for three days. Finally, they found Christ in the temple in the midst of the rabbis and teachers "and they were hearing him and asking him questions." (JST, Luke 2:46.) Immensely relieved and perhaps somewhat annoyed, Mary lovingly rebuked her son, saying, "Son, why hast thou thus dealt with us? behold, thy father and I have sought thee sorrowing." (Luke 2:48.) For the moment, Mary had forgotten whose son Christ was. But Christ had not forgotten. He knew who his Father was and he knew his Father was not searching frantically for him. Christ was in his Father's house doing his Father's business.

At twelve years of age, Christ understood he was the Son of God. However, he did not yet fully comprehend the great import of his mission.[13] This knowledge was gradually revealed to him as he progressed in grace and wisdom. Eventually, Christ had full knowledge and awareness of who he was and what he was to do. Neal A. Maxwell has said, "We do not know precisely when that full awareness occurred, but it surely preceded those special days of stress in the wilderness."[14]

Although we do not know exactly when Christ became aware of who he was, we know that this knowledge came to him, for early in his ministry Christ taught Nicodemus that He was the Son of God, that He would be crucified, and that He would ascend to His Father. When Christ cleared the temple the first time, he foretold of his resurrection. Christ testified to Mary, the sister of Martha and Lazarus, "I am the resurrection and the life: he that believeth in me, though he were dead, yet shall he live." (John 11:25.) Christ declared his divine origin and his mission to his apostles, his disciples, and his enemies. He proclaimed it in parables, rebukes, prophecies, and works. Undeniably, Christ knew who he was and what he was to do.

Surely, this knowledge gave Christ strength to withstand Satan's temptations, to endure the lack of faith of his own apostles, and to ignore the cruel mockery of the Roman soldiers. And in Gethsemane, when he was "sorrowful and very heavy" (see Matthew 26:37) and when he would rather not partake of the bitter cup, surely the knowledge of who he was and how important his mission was gave him strength to pray, "Not as I will, but as thou wilt." (Matthew 26:39.)

The knowledge of who we are and what we are to do can be a source of strength for us, just as it was for Christ. We are children of our Heavenly Father. We were begotten spiritually by him. He is our Father and from him and our Heavenly Mother we have inherited the seeds of divinity.

As his Spirit children, we were with him before this earth was created. We stood, like Abraham, before God among other noble and great spirits (see Abraham 3:22). And like Abraham, we were chosen for a great work. The Lord has made very clear through his prophets what this great work is. Spencer W. Kimball has stated that the "role of woman was fixed even before she was created, and God is the same yesterday, today, and forever." And this role, he explains, is first and foremost being a wife and mother. Truly, this is a great work. To be a wife and companion is so essential that it was for this reason that Eve was created (see Genesis, 2:18). This relationship is so important that God has revealed holy ordinances so that it can continue throughout the eternities.

Equally important is motherhood. President Kimball proclaimed motherhood to be "a holy calling, a sacred dedication for carrying out the Lord's work."[15] N. Eldon Tanner said, "One of [a woman's] greatest privileges, blessings, and opportunities is to be a co-partner with God in bringing his spirit children into the world."[16] And in 1942, the First Presidency of the Church stated, "Motherhood is near to divinity. It is the highest, holiest service to be assumed by mankind. It places her who honors its holy calling and service next to the angels."[17]

With this divine calling also comes tremendous responsibilities. We must teach our children to be obedient, honest, and chaste. We must teach them how to pray and repent. We must teach them the principles of the gospel and instill in them a knowledge of the scriptures. We must "train our children in our homes so completely in the way of right and truth that the destructive, godless philosophies and heresies of [the world] run off without penetrating, like water on a duck's back."[18]

This spiritual instruction weighs most heavily on us as mothers because we also have the greatest capacity for influence. Siegfried and Therese Engelmann, the authors of *Give Your Child a Superior Mind,* explained this when they wrote: "[A mother] will influence [her child's] attitudes and capacity to learn more than any other person in the world. . . . She will paint his emotions and help focus his eyes on what is 'important.' She is his most logical teacher."[19]

And so we see as Latter-day Saint women there is no greater responsibility or blessing than being a mother. This is the work the Lord has ordained for us to do. As we gain our own conviction of this, this knowledge will be a source of strength.

One day in correcting a sketch made by one of his pupils, the Russian artist Brulov added a stroke or two with his own brush. Immediately, the breath of life entered the painting. What had before been a very mediocre piece of work was transformed into a work of art. "My sketch is entirely changed," said the pupil, "and all you've done is to add a few strokes to it."

"The reason for that," answered Brulov, "is that Art entered the thing just where those strokes began."[20]

As we follow our Master's examples of prayer, scripture study, obedience, and knowing who we are and what we are to do, his hand will touch our lives. And just as the hand of the art master infused art into the amateur's painting, the touch of Christ will infuse spiritual strength into our souls. With this spiritual strength, we will have greater insight and wisdom; we will expand our ability to handle the demands of motherhood; and we will find greater joy and fulfillment as women, wives, and mothers.

NOTES

Chapter One:
Developing Personal Satisfaction

1. Epictetus, "The Golden Sayings of Epictetus," p. 171.
2. Fuller, ed., *2500 Anecdotes for All Occasions*, p. 127.
3. Dyer, *Pulling Your Own Strings*, p. 76.
4. "Self-Image, Ego Being Distorted," *Ogden Standard Examiner*, 27 Nov. 1980, p. 14G.
5. Rostand, *Cyrano de Bergerac*, pp. 50–51.
6. Thoreau, "Walden," p. 971.
7. Braude, *Handbook of Stories for Toastmasters and Speakers*, p. 377.
8. Smith, comp., *Teachings of the Prophet Joseph Smith*, p. 240.
9. Skinner, *Bartlett's Familiar Quotations*, p. 862.
10. Maugham, *Of Human Bondage*, p. 242.

Chapter Two:
Finding Satisfaction Amidst Failure

1. Braude, *Handbook of Stories for Toastmasters and Speakers*, pp. 359-60.
2. Fuller, ed., *2500 Anecdotes for All Occasions*, p. 427.
3. Von Oech, *A Whack on the Side of the Head*, p. 88.
4. Mandel, *A Complete Treasury of Stories For Public Speakers*, p. 3.
5. Braude, p. 156.
6. Blake, "Benjamin Disraeli," *Encyclopaedia Brittanica*, Macropaedia 5, pp. 899-900.
7. Adler, as quoted in "Facing Up to Failure," *Success*, November 1984, p. 51.

Chapter Three:
Defining Purpose and Direction

1. Fuller, ed., *2500 Anecdotes For All Occasions*, p. 15.
2. Shelley, *Frankenstein*, pp. 10–11, 56.

3. Saint-Exupery, *The Wisdom of the Sands*, p. 284.

4. Eyre, *A Joyful Mother of Children*, p. 45.

5. Ibid., p. 47.

Chapter Four:
Achieving Excellence and Self-fulfillment

1. Lewis and Wachs, *Best Jokes of All Time and How To Tell Them*, p. 142.

2. *1983 Goal Setting Guide*, p. A7.

3. Blanchard, *The One Minute Manager*, p. 31–32.

4. Von Oech, *A Whack On The Side Of The Head*, pp. 55–60.

5. Eyre, *The Discovery of Joy*, p. 111.

6. Tanner, "No Greater Honor: The Woman's Role," *Woman*, p. 9.

Chapter Five:
Attaining Happiness

1. Braude, *Handbook of Anecdotes by and about Famous Personalities*, p. 139.

2. Maltz, *Psycho-Cybernetics*, p. 95.

3. Anonymous.

4. Smith and Sjodahl, *Doctrine and Covenants Commentary*, p. 639.

5. McConkie, *Mormon Doctrine*, p. 791.

6. Chesley, *Seven Years in Hanoi*, p. 59.

7. Talmage, *Jesus the Christ*, p. 553.

8. Ibid., p. 558.

9. Plato, "The Apology of Socrates," pp. 18, 19.

10. Plato, "Crito," p. 31.

11. Tanner, "Integrity," *Ensign*, November 1977, pp. 16–17.

12. Dyer, *Gift from Eykis*, p. 121.

13. Cross, "Health Benefits of Laughter," *Encyclopaedia Britannica Instant Research Report*, p. 1.

14. Kimball, *Faith Precedes the Miracle*, p. 110-11.

15. Cross, p. 2.

16. Fuller, ed., *2500 Anecdotes for All Occasions*, p. 75.

17. Bombeck, *Motherhood the Second Oldest Profession*, pp. 130–31.

18. Braude, p. 41.

19. Maltz, p. 108.

20. Twain, *Bartlett's Familiar Quotations*, p. 624.

21. Mandel, *A Complete Treasury of Stories for Public Speakers*, p. 23.

22. Smith, comp., *The Teachings of the Prophet Joseph Smith*, p. 255.

Chapter Six:
Developing Spiritual Strength

1. Christensen, "Toward Greater Spirituality," *Ensign*, June 1983, p. 6.

NOTES

2. Madsen, *The Highest in Us,* p. 90.

3. Shakespeare, *Hamlet,* p. 943.

4. Iacocca, *Iacocca,* p. 47.

5. Condie, "And We Did Liken the Scriptures unto Our Marriage," *Ensign,* April 1984, p. 17.

6. Farrar, *The Life of Christ,* as quoted in James E. Talmage, *Jesus the Christ,* p. 81.

7. Romney, "Seek Not To Counsel the Lord," *Ensign,* August 1985, p. 5.

8. McConkie, *Mormon Doctrine,* p. 539.

9. Smith, *Gospel Doctrine,* p. 210.

10. Madsen, p. 49.

11. Talmage, *Jesus the Christ,* p. 22.

12. McConkie, p. 64.

13. Talmage, p. 123.

14. Maxwell, *Even As I Am,* p. 70.

15. Kimball, "The Blessings and Responsibilities of Womanhood," *Woman,* pp. 79, 80, 84.

16. Tanner, "No Greater Honor: The Woman's Role," *Woman,* p. 4.

17. Haight, "Woman As Mother," *Woman,* p. 19.

18. *Relief Society Courses of Study,* 1986, p. 3.

19. Engelmann, quoted in "Woman as a Teacher," *Woman,* p. 23.

20. Fuller, ed., *2500 Anecdotes for All Occasions,* pp. 220–21.

BIBLIOGRAPHY

Adler, Fred. As quoted in "Facing Up to Failure." *Success,* November 1984, pp. 48–52.

Barnet, Sylvan, ed. *The Complete Signet Classic Shakespeare.* New York: Harcourt, Brace, Jovanovich, Inc., 1972.

Blake, Robert Norman William. "Benjamin Disraeli." *Encyclopaedia Brittanica.* Macropaedia 5, 1983.

Blanchard, Kenneth, Ph.D. and Spencer Johnson, M.D. *The One Minute Manager.* New York, NY: Berkley Books, 1984.

Bombeck, Erma. *Motherhood the Second Oldest Profession.* New York, NY: McGraw-Hill Book Company, 1983.

Braude, Jacob M. *Handbook of Anecdotes by and about Famous Personalities.* Englewood Cliffs, NJ: Prentice-Hall, Inc., 1971.

———. *Handbook of Stories for Toastmasters and Speakers.* Englewood Cliffs, NJ: Prentice-Hall, Inc., 1951.

Chesley, Larry. *Seven Years in Hanoi.* Salt Lake City, UT: Bookcraft, 1973.

Christensen, Joe J. "Toward Greater Spirituality." *Ensign,* June 1983, pp. 6–9.

Condie, Spencer J. "And We Did Liken the Scriptures unto Our Marriage." *Ensign,* April 1984, pp. 17–20.

Cross, F. and W. "Health Benefits of Laughter." *Encyclopaedia Britannica Instant Research Report.* Chicago: IL, pp. 1–2.

Dyer, Wayne. *Gifts from Eykis.* New York, NY: Pocket Books, 1983.

———. *Pulling Your Own Strings.* New York, NY: Avon Books, 1977.

Engelmann, Siegfried and Therese. As quoted in "Woman as a Teacher." *Woman.* Salt Lake City, UT: Deseret Book Company, 1979.

Epictetus. "The Golden Sayings of Epictetus." trans. Hastings Crossley. *The Harvard Classics.* ed. Charles W. Eliot, LL.D. Danbury, CT: Grolier Enterprises Corp., 1980.

Eyre, Linda J. *A Joyful Mother of Children.* Salt Lake City, UT: Bookcraft, 1983.

Eyre, Richard. *The Discovery of Joy.* Salt Lake City, UT: Bookcraft, 1974.

Fuller, Edmund, ed. *2500 Anecdotes for All Occasions.* New York, NY: Avenel Books, 1980.

Haight, David B. "Woman As Mother." *Woman.* Salt Lake City, UT: Deseret Book Company, 1979.

Iacocca, Lee. *Iacocca.* New York, NY: Bantam Books, 1984.

Josephson, Matthew. "Thomas Alva Edison." *Encyclopaedia Brittanica.* Macropaedia 6, 1983.

Kimball, Spencer W. "The Blessings and Responsibilities of Womanhood." *Woman.* Salt Lake City, UT: Deseret Book Company, 1979.

————— *Faith Precedes the Miracle.* Salt Lake City, UT: Deseret Book Company, 1972.

Lewis, George Q. and Mark Wachs. *Best Jokes of All Time and How To Tell Them.* New York: Hawthorn Books, Inc., 1966.

Madsen, Truman G. *The Highest in Us.* Salt Lake City, UT: Bookcraft, Inc., 1978.

Maltz, Maxwell. *Psycho-Cybernetics.* New York, NY: Pocket Books, 1960.

Mandel, Morris. A Complete Treasury of Stories For Public Speakers. Middle Village, NY: Jonathan David Publishers, 1974.

Maxwell, Neal A. *Even As I Am.* Salt Lake City, UT: Deseret Book Company, 1982.

Maugham, W. Somerset. *Of Human Bondage.* New York, NY: Penguin Books, 1983.

McConkie, Bruce R. *Mormon Doctrine.* Salt Lake City, UT: Bookcraft, 1966.

1983 Goal Settings Guide. Chicago, IL: *Success Magazine,* 1983.

Plato, "The Apology of Socrates." trans. Benjamin Jowett. *The Harvard Classics.* ed. Charles W. Eliot, LL.D. Danbury, CT: Grolier Enterprises Corp., 1980.

————— "Crito." trans. Benjamin Jowett. *The Harvard Classics.* ed. Charles W. Eliot, LL.D. Danbury, CT: Grolier Enterprises Corp., 1980.

Romney, Marion G. "Seek Not To Counsel the Lord." *Ensign,* August 1985, pp. 2–5.

Relief Society Courses of Study 1986. Salt Lake City, UT: Church of Jesus Christ of Latter-day Saints, 1986.

Rostand, Edmond. *Cyrano de Bergerac.* trans. Lowell Bair. New York, NY: The New American Library, 1972.

Saint-Exupery, Antoine de. *The Wisdom of the Sands.* Chicago, IL: The University of Chicago Press, 1979.

"Self-Image, Ego Being Distorted." *Ogden Standard Examiner,* 27 November 1980, p. 14G.

Shelley, Mary. *Frankenstein.* New York, NY: Dell Publishing Co., Inc., 1975.

Skinner, B. F. As quoted in *Bartlett's Familiar Quotations.* Boston, MA: Little, Brown, and Company, 1980.

Smith, Hyrum M. and Janne M. Sjodahl. *Doctrine and Covenants Commentary.* Salt Lake City, UT: Deseret Book Company, 1978.

Smith, Joseph. *Teachings of the Prophet Joseph Smith.* comp. Joseph Fielding Smith. Salt Lake City, UT: Deseret Book Company, 1976.

Smith, Joseph F. *Gospel Doctrine.* Salt Lake City, UT: Deseret Book Company, 1978.

Talmage, James E. *Jesus the Christ.* Salt Lake City, UT: Deseret Book Company, 1970.

Tanner, N. Eldon. "No Greater Honor: The Woman's Role." *Woman.* Salt Lake City, UT: Deseret Book Company, 1979.

———— "Integrity." *Ensign,* November 1977, pp. 14–17.

Thoreau, Henry David. "Walden." *America in Literature.* ed. Theodore L. Gross. New York, NY: John Wiley and Sons, 1978.

Twain, Mark. As quoted in *Bartlett's Familiar Quotations.* Boston, MA: Little, Brown, and Company, 1980.

Von Oech, Roger, Ph.D. *A Whack on the Side of the Head.* Menlo Park, CA: Creative Think, 1983.

INDEX